1970 ELECTION

POWELL
and the
1970 ELECTION

edited by John Wood

A PAPERFRONT
ELLIOT RIGHT WAY BOOKS
KINGSWOOD, SURREY, U.K.

Made and printed by Cox & Wyman Ltd, London, Reading and Fakenham

CONTENTS

INTRODUCTION

Here, in full, and as delivered, are the five major speeches Mr. Powell made during the 1970 election, together with an account of the postbag they provoked and three brief essays tracing the course of the campaign, analysing the political forces at work and looking back at the behaviour of the polls.

This material is brought together to try to set the record straight, by making available some of the evidence needed to assess what influence Mr. Powell may have had. As is tentatively suggested by the contributors – and there can be no certainty about matters of this kind – it is at least possible that Mr. Powell played a decisive part in the unexpected Tory victory.

Such a conclusion conflicts with what was said at the time by most of the professional press, radio and television commentators. But the gap which they suppose to exist between Mr. Powell and Tory supporters in particular, or indeed public opinion in general, may more truly be a gap between themselves and the public.

In trying to understand the world around them people are increasingly suspicious of the confusion in much of the media between opinion making and straight reporting. There is growing resistance to the tendency of some journalists to influence rather than to inform. Moreover, efforts to belittle the great political alternatives as a trivial choice between – in Mr. Powell's words – 'a man with a pipe and a man with a boat', do not deceive millions of Britons who are deeply concerned about their country and wish serious issues to be discussed seriously.

In these circumstances what Mr. Powell has to say is listened to all the more intently and appears to provoke an unparalleled response. Certainly Mr. Cowling is right to say that Mr. Powell has changed the climate of opinion. In so doing, he has also reminded us that political platform speaking, if in the best tradition of reasoned debate and argument, can still have an impact on public thinking, even at election time.

JOHN WOOD

1

Mr. Powell, Mr. Heath, and the Future

by Maurice Cowling

Maurice Cowling is a Fellow of Peterhouse, Cambridge. Author of: '1867: Disraeli, Gladstone and Revolution', 'Mill and Liberalism', 'The Nature and Limits of Political Science'.

In a remarkable letter to the *Economist* ten days after the general election, Sir Edwin Leather* took to task the pollsters and pundits for not understanding that the Conservative party was going to win all along. Mr. Heath's victory was, he wrote, a victory for the 'ordinary people' who run the Conservative party up and down the country, who are 'un-news unless we commit murder or get involved in exceptionally juicy sex crimes' and who felt quietly pleased when it turned out that they had been right and the pundits wrong.

Sir Edwin of course is no more an 'ordinary person' than Mr. Hugh Cudlipp, Sir William Armstrong or the Chairman of the Independent Television Authority, but we may accept his view, for what it is worth, that 'the great big world of Fleet Street, Whitehall, St James's Street, the Television Centre and Shaftesbury Avenue' is 'out of touch' with 'the ordinary world' in which most people live,

* *Chairman of the National Union of Conservative Associations, 1969–70.*

and we may agree that, whatever happens to Mr. Heath in the future, he may now be spared the personal denigration he has had to suffer from some parts of these quarters in the past.

It is probably as well for Mr. Heath that his political courtship has been long and tricky and not marred, after too easy an acceptance in 1965, by easy acceptance thereafter. Europe clouds his future, as it clouds the futures of others. But he has now established an authority which has been greatly strengthened by the widespread illusion that he won because he staked out his line and stuck to his guns without trying to please anyone very much.

With all this, doubtless, Sir Edwin would agree. With the rest of this book, and with the belief that it is worthwhile to have a book on this subject, he would almost certainly not agree. For what was remarkable about his letter to the *Economist* was that, in the course of a 3,000-word analysis of the general election, he nowhere mentioned Mr. Powell, whose contribution was treated as though it did not exist.

From any point of view, this will not do. From the viewpoint of Conservatives seeking guidance about the future, it will not do at all. The future will be different, but Conservatives who seek guidance about it might as well know what the recent past was like. In particular they need to know whether the polls were as wrong as Sir Edwin wishes to believe, whether electors changed their minds in the final week and to what extent Mr. Heath and Mr. Powell, respectively, were responsible for the change, if there was one. In addition, they might ask whether the much-publicized concentration on marginal constituencies produced better results there than elsewhere, and whether Mr. Heath should best be seen as snatching victory from the jaws of defeat, or near-defeat from a position of almost unchallenged predominance a few months before the election was announced.

It is possible that the Conservative lead between 1967 and 1970 represented merely a recession in Labour support from which Labour recovered ten days before the election only to fall back again as Mr. Wilson's self-confidence became objectionable and the newspaper strike, food prices and the trade figures confirmed what Mr. Heath had been saying. Respect for Mr. Heath need not be reduced if his emphasis on the cost of living did not win the election by itself, if part of his difficulty at the beginning of the last week was caused by his quarrel with Mr. Powell and if his own campaign, flagging visibly, was given a boost by Mr. Powell in the latest stages notwithstanding. Whatever one may wish to believe, it is difficult to avoid the conclusion that Mr. Powell's impact on the election was great, that he made a strong appeal to many of the 'ordinary people' for whom Sir Edwin claims to speak, and that the two-year campaign he brought to an independent climax in the ten days before the election struck oil in places where Conservatives had not struck oil before.

What this book discusses is the evidence – the history of the election, the performance of the polls, the letters Mr. Powell received before and after Polling day and his election speeches.

The speeches should be read not just because they state a point of view but because of the inverse relationship between their heat and the heat generated by those who have attacked them. As in his other speeches there were passages to which some of Mr. Powell's admirers will not respond and thoughts which might have been better left unstated. But they justify neither reference (from Mr. Robert Blake) to their 'lunatic quality' nor Lord Poole's claim that the speeches were more 'intemperate' than any Mr. Powell had made before. They were not chiefly, as Lord Poole seems to suppose, about immigration. They were not intemperate. In general, as we shall see in a moment, they reflected a comprehensive sort of popular Conservatism which Conservatives who join in the attack (like Lord Poole and Mr. Blake) should take the trouble to recognize for what it is.

The letters confirm the existence of a body of opinion which those who respond to Mr. Powell need no external evidence to tell them existed, but they leave us guessing about its size. We know neither more nor less exactly than before how many people are alienated by Mr. Powell and how many attracted, on what scale he is listened to by people who listen to no other Conservative leader and in what numbers his words made Conservatives out of voters who would not have voted Conservative without them. Since we cannot be certain of the answers to any of these questions, we have for practical purposes to follow our noses while noting the fact, which the death of Mr. Macleod makes more important, that for most electors the Conservative party means Mr. Heath and Mr. Powell with only the shadowiest side-effects from Lord Hailsham, Mr. Maudling and Sir Alec Douglas-Home. In this connection, three things should be borne in mind.

The first is that Mr. Powell, so far from being a conventional figure of the Right, is capable both of batting all around the political wicket and of moving the stumps in order to set up a wicket of his own. His current doctrines are an intellectualized version of ideas which have been the common diet in most parts of the body of the Conservative party for the last 25 years, but they have been transformed in the course of exposition and given a wider range of relevance than they had before. In some respects they resemble the assumptions of the Monday Club except that they appeal neither chiefly to the middle classes nor mainly to members of the Conservative party and will be capable of greater flexibility in development once their centrality has been established. They are in fact the expression of a feeling, which is to some extent present in all classes, that the language used by politicians is not the language the body of the people understands and that the distance between politicians and the public is great and growing. Above all they confirm the impression that anyone who speaks a language the public wants to hear will attract the hysterical censure Mr. Powell has attracted from the self-appointed leaders of the 'thinking classes', i.e. the 'great big world of Fleet Street, Whitehall, St. James's Street', etc., etc., whose present mood Sir Edwin Leather is not alone in disliking very greatly.

13

Censure from this quarter is, however, an honourable wound, inflicted on Mr. Powell because he has undercut its confidence that public opinion will follow any lead it chooses to give. Mr. Powell has shown that the range of Conservative support can be extended even when its opinions are rejected. Most attempts at systematic rejection in the past have been made by politicians who lack intellectual stature. Nothing done by Mr. Powell has been more important than his demonstration that they can be rejected by a highly articulate thinking politician who attracts hysterical censure precisely because he rubs in the unpalatable truth that a rhetoric may be offensive to these parts of the 'thinking classes' and yet reflect opinions that are widely shared, deeply held and common to all classes in this country.

The second thing to notice is that, in this respect, Mr. Powell has been doing Mr. Heath's work for him. What Mr. Powell has done is to change the climate of opinion. This is a matter of great importance. Over the last thirty years a morally conservative, hard headed and patriotic electorate has been persuaded to defer to an eccentric element amongst the progressive intelligentsia with which it has nothing in common beyond the obscure conviction that the rich can have nothing in common with the rest. This has produced fear and intellectual uncertainty in the Conservative party and the presence in its higher reaches of a widespread belief that care should be taken to avoid a direct assault on the feelings and prejudices of this wing of the intelligentsia, however absurd the opinions to which it may be committed. Now that this period of deference seems to be coming to an end, Mr. Powell will make it easier for Mr. Heath to follow where a party leader might find it difficult to take a lead. In this connection the last election was encouraging. There need be no doubt that the next five years will give wider scope for repeating the pattern established over immigration, when Mr. Powell enabled Mr. Heath to present as an act of judicious moderation a policy which, if Mr. Powell had not eased his way with Labour voters, would have been stigmatized more successfully than it was as vile, racialist, Tory fascism.

The third thing to bear in mind is that in many respects Mr. Powell's and Mr. Heath's appeals are complementary, not conflicting. Both take seriously the threat from a militant body of opinion which is hostile to private concentrations of wealth, financial inequality and the existing form of mixed capitalism, as well as to the simple truths which give cohesion to the citizens of a nation-state. The appeal of this body of opinion is widespread and is always about to become more widespread still. In skilful or unscrupulous hands it could be a lever for a morally irresistible assault. In this respect Mr. Wilson's government was neither especially skilful nor particularly unscrupulous. In opposition it may sharpen the content of its attack and make it seem drabber, safer, more reputable and infinitely more dangerous than it has ever seemed before.

Mr. Heath's reaction has been to avoid the intellectual issue, to take his stand on competence, good nature and good-will and to imply that as much is being done as can reasonably be expected. Mr. Powell's reaction has been to attack the complacent near-Socialism of large parts of the official, intellectual and even managerial classes, to demand a general stiffening of intellectual fibre and to adopt positions which divide the intellectual leaders of the Labour movement from the body of Labour voters. Which tactic is more relevant to establishing a popular unity of national sentiment remains to be seen. Probably both are necessary. Major reductions in taxation joined with a major improvement in the economic climate in the next four years would do much to confirm the adequacy of Mr. Heath and his low-keyed confrontation. Failure to improve the economic climate would give a considerable stimulus to policies against which the Conservative party is designed to be a barrier. One of Mr. Powell's chief merits is that the attention he has revived so far – not only in relation to immigration – gives him a better chance of blunting class conflict propaganda, which remains the Labour party's strongest suit, presents the greatest threat to the Conservative party and is one of the most objectionable of political inventions.

Whether Mr. Powell will hold his audience is an open question. Mr. Heath's government will probably look good for a time and may turn out to be very good indeed. In opposition the Labour party may look very poor. Other factors may operate to make Mr. Powell seem querulous or anachronistic, including, just possibly, a lowering of the level of political tension. In all these matters one can do no more than guess. The guess that emerges from this book is that Mr. Powell will matter for a long time yet.

For all these reasons the lesson of the last election is that there should be an end to the pretence that Mr. Powell does not exist. No one grudges Mr. Heath his victory or doubts that he will be a serious and distinctive Prime Minister. No one expects his term of office to be a short one. But a major assault must be expected in the next three years and it will be necessary to consolidate the resources available in order to meet it. One such resource is Mr. Powell who can play a unique part in relation to the moral and intellectual assumptions from which the assault will be made. Even if there seems, tactically, something to be said, from Mr. Heath's point of view, for using Mr. Powell as a reactionary foil against which to highlight his own comparative enlightenment, he should hesitate to do so too often. He should hesitate because Mr. Powell may be in a position to bale the Conservative party out of a difficulty in the future and because, from a tactical viewpoint, it is far from clear that Mr. Powell will be the loser from being denied office until the government's honeymoon period is over. Europe and certain atmospheric effects inseparable from high-level political personality divide Mr. Heath from Mr. Powell, but they also have much in common. Both take their stand on national unity as the solvent of class conflict. Both have clear commitments against bureaucratic statism. Mr. Heath has office to demonstrate his political meaning, Mr. Powell a self-made political theatre. If Europe recedes as a political problem, there need really be nothing between them except differences of technique and irrelevant personal distaste. What this book shows is that it is not only Conservatives who want an end to a policy which excludes one of the twin Conservative leaders from the higher management of the Conservative party.

2

Enoch Powell's Election Letters

by Diana Spearman

Diana Spearman worked in the Conservative Research Department from 1948 to 1960. She was a Conservative Parliamentary Candidate at Hull in 1945. Author of: 'Modern Dictatorship', 'Democracy in England', *and* 'The Novel and Society'.

Enoch Powell received a large number of letters – between five and six thousand – during and immediately after the Election. About 60 letters, or just over 1 per cent, objected to statements made in the speeches, or reproached Powell for his views. Of the rest many declared either that the writers had voted Conservative because of his speeches or that they considered he had played a significant part in inducing the swing to the Conservatives which, according to the polls, must have taken place during the last few days before the election. Only one letter conveyed the contrary view. It was written by a defeated London Conservative candidate to his helpers, one of whom sent it to Powell with a strong expression to the contrary. This candidate maintained that Powell's speeches had affected him adversely – 'to put it in a nutshell, we would have won but for Enoch Powell's utterances on the one hand or the Liberal intervention on the other'.

It is obvious that these letters do not *prove* that

Powell made a significant contribution to the Conservative victory; to do this would require a vastly greater total, a sort of postal election. Nor do the letters provide the kind of evidence that can be obtained from a random sample. Random in this context means chosen at random or by chance. People who write letters explaining their political views are selected not by chance, but by a greater than average interest in politics.

The letters do, however, illustrate the impact of Powell's speeches, on a limited number of people certainly, but behind everyone who actually writes, there must be a number of others of the same opinion, who are too busy, too diffident or not energetic enough to compose, address and post a statement of their views. Both the usefulness of the letters and their limitations can, perhaps, best be realized if one thinks of the light that might, for example, be thrown on the election of 1906 or the impact of Joseph Chamberlain, if a collection of similar letters existed from those days.

As far as they go, the Powell letters tend to destroy various theories about the basis of Powell's influence. It has been suggested that his support comes mainly from places where there are no immigrants, where there is a large immigrant population, from the ignorant 'mob', or from the reactionary middle class.

The areas from which the letters come show that there is no substance in the first two ideas. Every region of England was represented, and a few places in Scotland and Wales, the farthest north being Inverness and the farthest south Penzance –

almost the proverbial 'John o'Groats to Land's End'. This at least indicates that Powell's impact was not confined to the Midlands. The counties producing the largest number of letters, apart from London – Lancashire, Staffordshire, Devonshire and Kent – do not seem to have any common characteristic. It must again be emphasized that the numbers are too small to provide a basis for any theory, but they are not compatible with the idea that only those in areas remote from the centres of immigration support Powell. Much less evidence is required to demolish than to construct a theory. It should also be noted that not all the letter writers are primarily interested in immigration. Powell's views on the Common Market, economic policy, law and order, and in one letter the preservation of the House of Lords, attracted votes to the Conservative party.

Every social class is represented, at least as far as class can be deduced from address, writing-paper and hand-writing (roughly speaking the more illegible the writing the higher the class). The spread between classes is perhaps best illustrated by the postal districts from which the London letters came, ranging from E.5 to S.W.1, from Ealing to Croydon, E.4, S.W.18, S.E.23, S.W.16, S.W.3, W.1 and many others.

Nor does it seem that Powell appeals to any particular age group. Age is more difficult to discover than class, but the very old and the very young (18 to 25) frequently mention their age, and if people have young children they often say so.

Powell supporters do not represent an economic

21

or a social class but an 'opinion' – opinion in the sense that early nineteenth-century democratic theorists thought of the word, when they supposed that, once the influence of landowners was destroyed, political factors would be based on opinion and not on economic interest.

The letter writers can be divided into two groups, those who declared that Powell's speeches had made a decisive contribution to the Conservative victory, and those who said that they themselves had been persuaded to vote Conservative by his speeches or television appearances.

It would be tedious to quote many from the first group because it would involve so much repetition, but some examples, illustrating the general tone, may be of interest.

Weybridge, Surrey.

'All your many supporters feel, I am sure, that the contribution of your speeches during the last week have made this wonderful victory possible, and it would appear that your words have not fallen on deaf ears after all.'

Chadwick End, Solihull.

'What pleasure it gives me to write to you today . . . to thank you, as an ordinary man in the street, for probably having had more to do with the Tory win than any other single person.'

Arborfield, Berks.

'There is no doubt in my mind that your efforts played a decisive part in the Tory victory.'

Norwich, Norfolk.

'Now it is all over, one can hear on every hand that you Enoch Powell won the Election for the Tories. On the 19th June at lunch time, I visited a half dozen pubs in the centre of Norwich and the topic was the Election and its result. The general view was that Enoch Powell had changed looming defeat into victory and people celebrated, in which I joined.'

Richmond, Virginia, U.S.A.

'On Tuesday prior to the election on Thursday, I returned to my home from London, having been in Britain since 6th May, except for one week in Austria. I was just about the only observer who predicted a Conservative victory (my forecast being a margin of 25 to 50 seats) and perhaps the only one to say that this would be almost entirely due to you. I insisted on this for weeks, right up to the day of departure, telling my pro-Conservative friends that their gloom was unwarranted; that the polls and pundits would fall flat on their faces: and that the actual results should prove to any objective analysts that Conservative victory would hinge largely upon the tremendous support for you among persons normally inclined to Labour, etc. . . . . My old friend, Sir Noel Hall, at Brasenose College, Oxford was the one person who disagreed with me concerning the impact you would have. He expressed the fear that you would cost the Conservatives the election. I insisted that their hopes for victory depended upon you.'

Shrewsbury, Salop.

'I have heard that at Oakengates there was a row of young socialist hecklers who were so impressed that after the meeting they left to vote Conservative.'

Old Sodbury, Glos.

'You have given the Conservatives a lot of votes and brought them back into power.'

Barbican, London, E.C.2.

'Your integrity and courage I was convinced from the beginning would make a major contribution to a Conservative victory.'

Okehampton, Devon.

'Your magnanimity I feel sure was a major factor in swinging masses of the electorate back on to the proper course from which they so sadly deviated since 1966.'

Cardiff.

'We feel you brought the campaign to life for the Conservative Party and set us all on the road to success.'

Dumbarton.

'You have helped the Conservative cause tremendously.'

St. Andrews, Fife.

'When you started to speak up again during the election campaign I then began to think there was a hope we might win. I was profoundly relieved. Of course, it will be impossible to be sure exactly why the tide did turn in our favour so late, but I can't help thinking your words had much to do with it.'

Warstock, Birmingham, 14.
'I feel I must write to congratulate you on the tremendous impact of your campaign. Your eve-of-poll [i.e. 16th June] speech was simply magnificent and in its effect on people like myself was probably the decisive factor in the result nationally.'

Bradford.
'I wish to state that in my opinion your election speech which contained "the enemies within" was the greatest speech I have heard in a statesmanlike manner since the days of wartime Churchill. This was where the tide began to turn in the Conservatives' favour ... I believe the Conservative Party would have been defeated the week before ... If Mr. Heath had not given his good speech this week, but above all without your intervention all would have been lost.'

Falmouth.
'Was it the "Voice of Enoch"? It most certainly was! I have been a Conservative all my life, but I was depressed the day the Polls gave a 12 per cent Labour lead. The lunch-time World at One were mouthing obituary notices for the Tory Party and I longed for Enoch to rouse the

Nation. And he did. Bob Mellish, the Labour Whip, Jennie Lee, Jeremy Thorpe, all say it was Mr. Powell. They should know! Thank you, Mr. Enoch Powell.'

Witton, Birmingham, 6.

'I would just like to thank you on behalf of myself and many more people for making it possible for the Conservative Party to win the election. To the charge that you "stabbed Mr. Heath in the back" we would say that the knife must have been very blunt, for all it did was to push him straight through the door of No. 10 Downing Street.'

St. Helens, Isle of Wight.

'My wife and I would like to offer our most sincere congratulations for the great help you gave to the Conservative Party which contributed a tremendous moral influence towards its successful conclusion.'

Barnet, Herts.

'I must thank you for your speeches during the election campaign. These courageous speeches, and the Conservative victory which you helped to achieve, have, at least for the present, saved us from the creeping tide of anarchy . . . I say this not as a Conservative but a Liberal voter.'

Sutton Green, Guildford, Surrey – to Mr. Cranley Onslow.

'One compelling reason for my vote for you

was my conviction that this country's best hopes in the difficult times ahead lie in having your colleague, Mr. Enoch Powell, at the helm. Ergo, I voted Tory (much as I detest the monolithic party system) with the hope of seeing your party win and the hope that Mr. Powell will soon succeed Mr. Heath as leader of the party and as Prime Minister.'

Copied to Mr. Enoch Powell, with the comment: 'Till recent years, God forgive me, I was a staunch Labour supporter. Last month I voted Tory for the first time in the hope (slight, I fear) of having you as Prime Minister in the near future.'

When the letter-writers speak from their experience as canvassers or as local party officials their evidence clearly carries more weight.

Nuneaton.
'The favourable effect which Mr. Powell's television appearances and especially his final Plea to vote Conservative had on many wavering voters, was noted by members of the Branch from canvassing and follow-up interviews with voters and also from general conversation in the district.'

Luton, Beds.
'During canvassing here in Bedfordshire, I can assure you that hundreds of people voted for the Conservative party, indeed it must be said thousands of people, in support of yourself.'

Painswick, Glos.

'Despite a tendency to belittle your intervention in the election campaign, there is absolutely no doubt that yours was the deciding voice for many people.

'As a canvasser and as a teller, I can vouch for the fact that literally hundreds of people changed their minds and decided to vote "for Enoch". It was said on the door-step and after they left the polling booth.'

Wellington, Salop.

'The interest that was aroused by your visit may well have made all the difference to the result of the Election here ... Thank you for coming to the Wrekin. Eight hundred people came away from it inspired, full of enthusiasm, and in several cases that I have heard of, completely converted from Socialism to Conservatism.'

Exeter.

'Our canvassing has proved overwhelming support for what you are saying.'

Thornton Heath, Surrey.

'Those of us who worked in Midlands (particularly West Midlands) constituencies know that you contributed significantly to the Party's victory'.

Two defeated Labour ex-members of Parliament, Woodrow Wyatt in Bosworth and Jennie Lee in Cannock, appear to have shared these impressions; for they are reported to have attributed their defeat to the effect of 'Powellism'.

In many ways the letters from people who decided to vote Conservative on Powell's advice conveyed in his speech of 16th June, or (once or twice) in a private letter, are of more interest than the more general statements. Examples are given below.

Blakeney, Holt, Norfolk.
'It was my intention never to vote for the Conservative Party again . . . but in view of your recent appeal, I shall vote Conservative.'

Taunton, Somerset.
'. . . . if you wish it (and apparently you do), we will vote for the local Conservative candidate, but with little enthusiasm.'

Ardleigh, Essex.
'But for your final speech, I would not have bothered to vote.'

King's Cross Road, London, W.C.1.
'I was half inclined not to vote Tory after the way you had been treated and to abstain, but after your great "Vote Tory" speech, I decided to vote and I, needless to say, voted Tory. You certainly did tip the balance in favour of the Tories.'

Kensington, London, W.8.
'I shall vote for the Tory Party tomorrow

as you have asked – but this is the only reason. My first reaction was to abstain, and I am sure my opinion is shared by 90 per cent of this country.'

Acton, London, W.3.
'We did as you advised and all voted Tory.'

Chelmsford, Essex.
'I only voted Conservative because I felt I was voting for you . . . and 14 other supporters.'

Gateshead, 9.
'Various customers of mine of many walks of life from the shipyard workers to the company director tell me that they voted Tory because of Enoch Powell. Surely your fellow compatriots must know that Mr. Heath would never have pulled off this election on his performance alone.'

Styvechale, Coventry.
'You were right to assume that your speeches on certain subjects helped people in their decision to vote in spite of their doubts. Many, like myself, were going to abstain on 18th June.'

Hammersmith, London, W.6.
'I, probably like lots more, voted Conservative because I agreed with your views and the Conservative party was your lane along which you could get your views carried.'

Highgate, London, N.6.

'Thank you for your letter [urging "vote Tory"] ... I have this morning received from 32 Smith Square a copy of "The Common Market: Implications for Britain" ... I am acknowledging the receipt of the booklet, together with a copy of his Election Manifesto, and at the same time informing him [Mr. Heath] that if I do change my mind about voting, it will be entirely due to your request that I do so.'

Surlingham, Norwich – to Mr. Ian Gilmour.

'Tomorrow you will have the votes of this household, but I think it right to tell you that we, and hundreds of thousands of others throughout the land who think as we do, will be casting a reluctant vote.

'Our vote will be a reluctant one chiefly because of the incredibly unfair way in which leading Conservatives have treated Mr. Enoch Powell and the virtual election promise of Mr. Heath not to give him a cabinet post if the Conservatives are returned to power; for, make no mistake about it, if the Conservatives win the General Election, it is to Mr. Powell that our gratitude must flow.'

Brigg, Lincs.

'On a busy night when I otherwise would not have voted, since it made no difference, I made time to go to the polls, and, roused by Wedgwood Benn's immoderate attack on you, I placed my cross not for the Conservative candidate, not for the party of Ted Heath, but, in sympathy with you, for the party of Enoch Powell.

'I suspect there are many more like me in constituencies where it did count who did the same. Hence the victory.'

Beeston, Notts.

'I've always been a Conservative even though a working man, though never a party member. Rest assured as a result of your wonderful efforts on our behalf I'm joining ... Rest assured we have no doubts who is responsible for Conservative victory; it's yourself.'

Anglesey.

'I admire and trust Mr. Heath, but believe that he won largely because your philosophy and brave stand in the face of abuse and ridicule struck a note which inspired a majority of voters with a sense of confidence and courage they have not felt for years. I belong to that majority – the silent majority, hidden and forgotten, largely ignored – I mean the English, white, protestant. We have had no spokesman for decades, no organization, no party, we do not organize, we have no popular folklore, and our sense of nationalism is muted to a degree that its voice can hardly be heard. But we are a vast majority and we have responded to your voice.'

Hassocks, Sussex.

'I pray that Mr. Heath may realize how much of his success he owes to you. All my life I have been a Conservative but I would like you to know that my vote this time (for Lewes constituency) was cast primarily in support of you. There must be thousands like me throughout the country . . . All due praise to Mr. Heath, but without you I feel that no such victory could have been achieved.'

Bristol, 7.
'I am convinced (from my own opinion poll with my neighbours) that this Conservative triumph is entirely due to you. In the case of my family it definitely is: we were so disgusted when you were sacked from the shadow cabinet that we vowed never to vote for Heath – we only voted because you advised us all to do so. I made this quite clear to our candidate.'

Crewe, Cheshire.
'It was only Mr. Enoch Powell's appeal to vote for the Conservative Party that made me cast my vote for the Tories.'

Scotstown, Glasgow, W4.
'On reading my *Daily Express* on 17th June, and you telling me no matter whether my party have cast me off, go out tomorrow and vote Tory, I did just that, but my one regret, Sir, was that your name was not on my ballot paper.'

Clayton, Manchester.
'I had made up my mind not to go to the polls

for the first time in 36 years . . . It is entirely due to your appeal in this morning's *Daily Express* for the people to support Mr. Heath, give him your full support, that is why tomorrow, Mr. Powell, I will be at the Polls giving my vote once again for the 37th year to the Tory Party. This will also indirectly affect 25 other members of our family and also friends.'

Beeston, Notts.

'I am 69. Up to 1965 [1966?] I had always voted Tory, but this time I had decided not to vote at all – until I heard your latest speech saying "vote Tory".'

Falmouth, Cornwall – to the Chairman of the Conservative Party.

'Tomorrow I shall vote Conservative, in obedience to Mr. Enoch Powell's instructions. It is not a vote for Mr. Heath, but a vote belonging to Mr. Powell. If the Conservatives get in, it will be thanks to Mr. Powell. I have no means, other than writing to you, to make plain that tomorrow in voting for David Mudd, I am in reality casting it for the true leader of England, Enoch Powell, the guardian of its virtue.'

West Harrow, Middlesex

'In accordance with your advice and wishes, I will vote for our Conservative candidate to-morrow, altho' it was my intention either not to vote at all, or to write your name upon my paper – thus spoiling it, I know.'

Strelley Estate, Nottingham.

'We are only still voting Conservative because you ask us to; otherwise we would have refrained from voting as a protest to all who oppose you.'

Walton, Liverpool.

'At your request, but with great reluctance, myself, wife, and family will probably vote for the Conservative Party.'

Sale, Cheshire.

'Mr. Barber will be told that he is getting our votes as a tribute to you, not Mr. Heath (who should be leading the Liberal Party).'

Temple Gardens, London, E.C.4.

'I shall vote Tory tomorrow because you have asked me to. I shall resign from the Party after the Election.'

Ramsbottom, Bury, Lancashire.

'I would not have voted this time, but for what you have said ... I know a lot in Ramsbottom, they were not going to vote this time but for you.'

Sale, Cheshire.

'I wrote to you when they threw you off the "Shadow Cabinet". You wrote to me telling me to still support the party policy – as I felt at that time I could not. This I have done.'

Garstang, Lancs.

'Thank you very much for your help and advice in this morning's mail ... I shall vote as you have advised.'

Long Eaton, Nottingham.

'I voted Conservative today only because you said to.'

Earl's Court, London, S.W.5.

'I did not intend to vote at all; but when I thought of your appeal to vote Conservative, in spite of my personal dislike of Mr. Heath, I voted for him and persuaded family and friends to do likewise.'

Morden, Surrey.

'I got your message; so voted after all "for a free country, and great because it is free".'

Hurley, Maidenhead.

'Your directive to your supporters to vote Conservative absolved me from my publicly stated vow not to vote Conservative unless you were reinstated in the Shadow Cabinet. Mine was therefore one vote you got for the Conservative Party.'

Southampton.

'I have not voted for any party since Mr. Baldwin was elected Prime Minister ... I trust there are a great number of people in your constituency who would think the same as me and give you their votes.'

Whitechapel Road, London, E.1 – to Mr. Heath.

'I shall vote Conservative only because Enoch, with the loyalty you lack, asked for that, but I shall not vote a second time for a party with a leader of whom I am ashamed.'

Kingsbury, London, N.W.9.

'I would like to tell you that at least 65 per cent of my workmates are Tories and I know that several of them, including a Labour follower, voted Tory simply as a gesture of their great respect for your goodself.'

Kempston, Bedford.

'The comment in one of the national papers was right – we are going to vote for the Conservatives, simply because you are one of them.'

Leeds.

'Congratulations on your tremendous success ... around the whole country. You were responsible for my Conservative vote and many of my friends' votes.'

Bridgwater, Somerset.

'I voted Tory because you asked us to do so!'

Beckenham, Kent.

'I had not intended to vote at all ... I wrote across my official polling card which I handed to the Conservative teller – "and you can thank Mr.

Enoch Powell for my vote". It's my guess you added millions to the Conservative vote. My husband, who hasn't voted for forty years, voted Conservative too.'

Upminster, Essex.
'I would like you to know that I voted Conservative after listening to you.'

Bishop Auckland, Co. Durham.
'I was impatient with the suggestion that your speeches were damaging the Tory vote: on the contrary, many people voted Conservative because you belong to our Party. Labour supporters envied us.'

Blackburn, Lancs.
'It is on *your* account, and *your* policy on immigration and the Common Market, we shall vote Conservative.'

Edinburgh, 3.
'I shall vote Conservative largely because you, Mr. Powell, have got down to the real issues with which a future government should be dealing.'

Colchester, Essex.
'We are voting Tory just for you. Thank you.'

Binley, Coventry.
'Had you not put up for Parliament, I and many of my friends would not have voted.'

Exeter.

'I took your advice – as many others must have done – and voted Conservative, and am delighted with the result.'

Fairwater, Coventry.

'Your letter to me was a great help during the election campaign. Many people that felt as I did about withholding my vote were given your advice. In the end I carried your letter with me, and quite a few people read it. I am sure that you brought in more votes for the Conservative party than any other single person, and I am only speaking for a very small part of the country. When you spoke on the 16th June and was accused of stabbing your leader in the back, I said to a friend next day: We are going to win this election. Mr. Heath will now get through "because of" not "in spite of" what Mr. Powell has been saying at all his meetings.'

Smith Street, London, S.W.3.

'As hardened old Tory voters, we feel bound to tell you that we were waverers. Then came your speech before the Election. We promptly plumped for Worsley. This can therefore add two more to the file: "Those who voted Tory because of me".'

The above quotations are from letters that appear to be written by persons of Conservative inclination, even when this is not expressly stated. There were also a number from voters who had previously been Labour or Liberal.

Tipton, Staffs.

'I am a staunch Labour supporter. Yesterday for the first time ever in my adult life I put a X by a Conservative Candidate mainly because of your campaign on Race Relations.'

Bournemouth, Hants.

'This family has always voted Labour (4 votes), but as a demonstration of support for yourself, we all voted Conservative.'

Swanage, Dorset.

'I am a Liberal as were my father and grandfather . . . I am voting Tory as you decide it is best for England.'

Brook, Nr. Godalming, Surrey.

'Like so many of my ex-G.P.O. colleagues and friends who have always supported Labour, I voted Conservative for the first time in my life because we feel you are the only M.P. who has shown enough courage to speak up for us and for this you have won thousands of admirers all over the country. All sorts of excuses will be made about how the Conservatives achieved victory; but we, your supporters, can assure you that you can take more than half the credit for this achievement.'

Harrow, Middlesex.

'I voted Tory for the first time because I agree with your views on immigration.'

Folkestone.

'Life-long Labour supporter – who voted Conservative on this issue [immigration] alone.'

Swindon, Wiltshire.

'The Tories have had my vote for the first time in my life.

'Had decided to abstain from voting until Wednesday evening, when I managed to read the full report of your speech in the *Sunday Express* front page ... Voted this morning, and now reading today's *Daily Express,* and note that "Powell: 'I've won over votes for Tories'" headline. You are so right.'

Bootle.

'I am just going to cast my vote for Conservative ... but Sir I am voting for the Rt. Hon. Enoch Powell. I have always voted Labour; but with such a great man (A REALIST) in the opposition, it leaves me no choice.'

Bury St. Edmund's, Suffolk.

'Although I have always voted Labour – I shall cast my vote for the Conservative candidate this time ... Had it not been for your statements (so very true), I'd have wasted my vote on Labour, or refrained once again.'

Ilford, Essex.

'I am merely one of the throng, an engineer, and have voted both Labour and Tory in the past and this time would not have voted but for your realistic views which coincide with those of most of us.'

Westbourne Grove, London, W.2.
'I voted Conservative because of my belief in you.'

Wolverhampton, S.W.
'It looks very much like a Conservative government by the early results; but I am hoping that this is not true, as I am a Socialist but not a member of the Labour party. Your outspoken views on the colour question has helped the Conservative party, not hindered it ... The person the Labour party had to fear was you.'

Alderley Edge, Cheshire.
'For the first time in my life I voted Conservative in this election. I would like you to know that I did this because it was the only way I could show how much I admire your great courage and how much I agree with your views.'

Carlisle.
'I have voted Labour for a great number of years now but at this present election I voted for the Conservative Party. My main reason for doing this was because you in your speeches were voicing my opinions and as a loyal member of Britain and a great believer in Britain I could do no other. I have written to the Prime Minister, Mr. Heath, in this vein and also stated that I

think he owed his success to your firm stand on the immigrant problem.'

Kentish Town, N.W.5 – to Mr. Harold Wilson.
'All my life I have voted for Labour. So did my late husband, who died in August last year. For the first time in my life I voted Conservative this time. Why did I change my mind? I'm sure you will be interested to know the answer to that question and I think I owe you an explanation. I'm a "charlady" aged 59, who earns £6-12-0 a week. I changed my mind and voted Conservative – not because I like Mr. Heath, in fact I don't care for him very much at all, – because I agree with Mr. Enoch Powell on the immigration issue, because of the housing problem and because of the increase in prices. In that order.'

Billericay, Essex.
'With my life history, going back to bitter childhood memories of the Depression in the North, I would never have believed that I could ever bring myself to vote Tory. Last week I did just that. I did it because your Tory voice is the only one to speak out and at least give an airing to this huge problem [immigration].'

Harpenden, Herts.
'Mainly due to your outspoken sincerity and practical sense, which I believe won your party many seats, my vote (recently Liberal – in a safe Conservative constituency) was firmly Tory.'

43

London, E.12.

'I would like to bring to your notice, that I only voted Tory at the last Election because you advised me to.'

North Shore, Blackpool.

'I have voted and worked for the Labour party for twenty years, and you have helped me to change my views.'

Fulham, London, S.W.6.

'After 25 years of voting Labour I have now voted for the Tories, but not for Mr. Heath or any of his cabinet. I voted in support of you, Sir, of you as a man, and for your views.'

Chelsea, London, S.W.3.

'All my friends in different parts of London voted Conservative, only because of you.'

Acton, London, W.3.

'Mr. Heath and the Conservative Party can thank you alone for their narrow victory over Wilsonian Socialism. When you appealed to your supporters that we were not to abstain, but to vote Conservative, for the future benefit of the country, I – like millions of others of similar opinions – obeyed your advice.'

Brookmans Park, Herts.

'As a voter who has never been committed to any one Party I should like to let you know that I supported the Tories at last week's election because you are one of its members. For the same reason a number of my friends did likewise and, as a result of some random inquiries made since last Friday, I believe that your eve-of-poll speech was a decisive factor in determining the fate of the Socialist Administration.'

South Ockendon, Essex.

'As a firm supporter of Labour for many years, I have now gone over to Tories, thanks to you and your policies.'

Corby, Northamptonshire.

'I am 66 years of age, of life-long leanings to Labour, my parents were Labour, indeed the whole family were ... but now I am for the first time going to vote Conservative. You and your stand on immigration has brought this about.'

Leeds.

'We come from an old Socialist family, not the Left-Wing or Communist type, but today we voted Tory and our family also ... Our feeling for our country took precedent over any personal gains in betterment for this or that, and you inspired us further to be true to what we were really feeling.'

Plymouth.

'Thank you and good luck to your efforts from a Plymouth Hoe ex-Labour supporter.'

St. Albans, Herts.

'I influenced many people to vote Conservative, as I firmly believe you to be right in your statements. Many of these people had originally no intention of voting.'

Farnworth, Lancs.

'There is no doubt in my mind that you and you alone swung the Election in favour of your Party ... I just took your words for what they were, the truth. That is why I and millions of other Labour voters who could not vote for you directly did the next best thing and voted Conservative. Finally I am convinced that you were the kingpin in the Election.'

Ilford, Essex.

'Thank you for your letter of the 27th May. I waited before replying because I was wavering between you and the National Front candidate who stood for Ilford South. As this could be nothing more than a protest vote this time, I finally decided to vote Tory, but only because you asked me to.'

Blackpool.

'I have worked and voted for the Labour party for 20 years, and you have helped to change my views.'

Ealing, London, W.5.

'Thank you for what you have done for Britain. Your courage and honesty has won a lot of people like myself to the Conservatives.'

Brighton.

'Thank you Mr. Powell, for your courageous speech – my vote will be changed from Labour to one for Conservative.'

The nature and extent of Powell's contribution to the Conservative victory must remain a matter of opinion as it is impossible to produce the kind of evidence which would convince anyone who was resolutely sceptical. What follows is no more than my own personal view.

From reading not only a proportion of the election letters but also some four thousand of the scores of thousands of letters written to Powell after his speech on immigration at Birmingham in 1968 (analysed in 'Enoch Powell's Postbag', *New Society*, 27th June, 1968), it is my conclusion that he has a considerable following, bound together, as has been previously suggested, not by class, economic or social, or by geography, but by an attitude to politics. They are, I think, intensely patriotic in the sense that they value British culture and traditions and are angered by the continuous denigration of them in so much of the communications media (which may make them less sensitive to wide international issues). They are also intensely democratic, not so much in the sense that they hold any particular theory, but they take pride in the democratic nature of British institutions, which should enable them to take a part, even if a small part, in political decisions. And although professors, doctors, lawyers and other intellectuals are numbered among Powell's supporters, they are democratic also in that none of them have the typical intellectual's contempt for the 'uneducated', the 'ignorant mob'. Working man and professional man alike feel that the democratic procedure is stultified by the attitude of established authorities, party leaders, church dignitaries and civil servants. In many of them this attitude is shown in the phrase, so often heard, 'we must face the fact that Britain is now a multi-racial society'. They argue that to take a decision to make the country multi-racial was momentous, and if democracy has any meaning should have been pronounced on by the electorate. More sophisticated observers may think this is a naïve view, because in reality no such decision was ever made.

In the eyes of Powell's supporters exactly the same disregard of the democratic process seems to be taking place over the Common Market. Another complaint is the way in which so many politicians talk down to the electorate, shrouding their real opinions on any controversial problem under a veil of respectable platitudes. One of the main sources of Powell's appeal is that people feel he is speaking to them as equals, as adult participants, even if on a different level from himself, in the process of democratic government. Phrases and sentiments which shock consensus opinion make them believe he is sharing his thinking with them. Some of his correspondents who do not support any of his views have expressed their appreciation of this frankness.

Many factors no doubt contributed to the Conservative victory – as they do to every historical event – among them Heath's unshaken confidence in the face of all discouragement, the publication of the trade figures, and Wilson's arrogance. But I find it impossible to resist the impression that without the impact of Powell's speeches, although the victory would possibly have been won, the size of the majority would have been smaller.

3

The 1970 Election Campaign

by George Gale

The electoral situation when the Prime Minister's decision to go to the country was announced on 18th May was confusing. From the middle of 1967 until April 1970, the indications both of polls and of by-elections and local government election results had been for a Tory victory. This very persistent Conservative lead throughout 1968, 1969 and the early months of 1970 had varied widely and indeed wildly, see-sawing for reasons that were never convincingly explained. But suddenly, at the end of April and more especially in the first fortnight of May, local government election results and polls suggested, almost miraculously from Labour's point of view, the prospect of a Labour victory. The principal reasons adduced for the rise in Labour's popularity, which encouraged Wilson to envisage electoral success, were first the image supposedly produced by the February conference of Conservatives at Selsdon Park Hotel, of an 'abrasive', 'bashing', 'radical' party seeking to bring about 'change'; second, Roy Jenkins' Budget which, by making no great changes in the tax structure, was widely interpreted as an 'honest' and 'brave' refusal to produce an 'electioneering' budget (which, in effect, it therefore presumably was: for an 'electioneering' budget, by giving away too much, would have been condemned as dishonest and irresponsible, and therefore an electoral liability); and third, and probably quite the most important, the improvement in the balance of payments figures which appeared to show to an electorate conditioned for years to regard these figures as the test of the country's performance and success, that the country at long last was managing to pay its way.

Such was the electoral situation, what of the general state of affairs? The principal problem confronting the Government was Northern Ireland. In so far as this impinged electorally, it did so to Labour's advantage. First, because of the general respect accorded to Callaghan, for his handling of it as Home Secretary; second, because Paisleyite intervention in contesting Ulster Unionist seats could only embarrass and lose seats for the Conservative Party; and third, because the Irish vote in England, almost entirely Catholic and Labour, but usually apathetic, could be expected this time, and for the first time, to vote at something near its full strength. But neither the Labour nor the Conservative Party was disposed to make of Northern Ireland an electoral issue, since the leaders of both parties knew perfectly well the intractable nature of that problem and had no desire to make their positions worse, should they succeed to power.

The chief concern abroad was the Common Market negotiation. Here, again, the leadership of neither party was disposed, or in a position, to make much of an issue of it. Of all British politicians of the first rank, Heath, who had himself conducted the previous negotiations, was the foremost marketeer. But Wilson, despite some wobblings, had set in motion the present negotiations. The application, was a (Labour) Government initiative and policy supported by the (Conservative) Opposition and accepted, with much private misgiving, by both parties. The Liberal Party, which on historical grounds as well as on grounds of electoral advantage, might have been expected to be most hostile to the idea of joining a Continental Closed Shop, had long since been committed to excessive enthusiasm for the European tariff system by its one-time leader, Mr. Jo Grimond, and his more human but no less misguided successor, Mr. Jeremy Thorpe. The evidence of the polls was that the country at large was moving more and more against the Common Market; but with the leadership of all parties agreed, supported by most commentators and most of the Press, there existed no political way in which existing public opinion could express itelf or be expressed. The Common Market negotiation can, therefore, best be described at this time as a topic rather than a political or partisan issue.

Foreign policy seldom plays much of a part in British elections, and, the Common Market apart, only two aspects of foreign policy need be mentioned, both because of their by-products. Wilson's Rhodesian policy annoyed right-wingers and many (largely Scots) with Rhodesian kith and kin. It was essentially a failed policy; and Heath was prepared to talk again with Ian Smith. Nevertheless a good deal of bi-partisan consensus remained, for Sir Alec Douglas-Home had first enunciated the 'five principles', to which Wilson had added a sixth of no great significance, but, as it were, for good measure. The Rhodesian question remained capable of arousing heat and anger; and to the extent that Wilson was colder towards Smith than Heath, and to the extent that Wilson's policy of sanctions (although endorsed by the Conservatives) had failed, a marginal advantage can be said to have accrued to the Conservatives here.

This advantage may well have been augmented by the disadvantage to Labour of Wilson's continuing support of the United States' position in Vietnam, and, more briefly but possibly not less disastrously, in Cambodia. Here again Wilson's policy was also Conservative policy. But whereas few Conservatives felt unduly revolted at the spectacle of a British Labour Government supporting the American position, a great number of Socialists felt outraged. Wilson was to attract much more anger than Heath during the campaign. The same, generally, could be said of Labour candidates. The anger came almost entirely from their own people and those to their left. Further, the frequently screened sight of left-wing demonstrations, albeit against the Labour Government, must be presumed to have told against the Government whose party was the more readily associated with protest.

By and large Britain had not exercised or possessed much in the way of a foreign policy throughout the sixties; and I incline to the view that the Catholic anger produced by Britain's acquiescence in Nigeria's suppression of the Biafran revolt, although genuine among a small and familiar group of intellectuals of the Right and useful to the agitators of the Left, was altogether less electorally or socially significant than the Catholic anger produced by Ireland. It was, however, an aspect of disaffection.

Since 1968 one university after another had provided spectacles of student protests and violence. Any demonstration tended to be against the Government; and violence thus ensuing tended to be a failure of governance. The rioting in America, France and Germany, which began in 1968, continued throughout 1969 and into 1970. The question of 'Law and Order' was raised on all sides, but not answered.

The movement towards 'the Permissive Society' had progressed steadily in the years of the Labour Government through relaxation or abolition of the legal penalties for murder, buggery, abortion, suicide, and obscene publications, and through the reduction of impediments to divorce. Then the full frontal nude arrived at about the same time as the General Election. And although none of this tolerable, and in most cases, welcome libertarianism ever became specific as an election issue, it was very much part and parcel of the same diffuse debate on 'Law and Order'. Those who disliked demonstrations also disliked the 'Permissive Society', wished for more Law and certainly better Order, and expected to have their wishes better met by a Conservative than by a Socialist Government.

There was thus disaffection with the Government both from the right and from the left; and although in the judgment of subsequent historians this may help to establish the success Wilson had had in capturing the centre, at a time of election the effect was to discourage the activists of the Left, and to encourage those of the Right.

The largely covert hostility between both groups of activists looked as if it might become overt in the weeks preceding the election, and serious and widespread disorder ensue, thanks to an issue which might well have dominated the General Election, to the presumed great disadvantage of the Labour Party. This issue, which fused the more general issues of race, of political protest, and of 'Law and Order', in a peculiarly English way and in a fashion which all could readily discuss, was the proposed South African cricket tour. The tour might well have proceeded without much fuss and have afforded much cricketing pleasure, but for the determination of young activists led by Mr. Peter Hain and Mr. Louis Eaks to have the tour called off. Their ability to lay on demonstrations was not in doubt. Throughout the spring the defence of cricket grounds where the Springbok tourists were scheduled to play was discussed, planned and put into effect. Threats were made not only to demonstrate but to prevent play or to disrupt it, and it was these threats, neither lightly made nor lightly taken, which transformed the issue: for the risk of grave rioting between spectators and demonstrators was real. Moreover, much rioting would undoubtedly acquire a racial tone; for the ostensible objection to the South African cricketers was to do with the policy of apartheid.

On the eve of the Election, the temperature of the country was rising fast; and, chiefly as a result of the movement to Ban the Tour, it was the racial issue which was doing the over-heating. It is no exaggeration to say that from the beginning of 1968 until the General Election the question of race and the name of Powell were inseparable. The presences and absences of Powell dominated the 1968 and 1969 Conservative Party conferences at Blackpool and Brighton. Powell, in terms of popular reaction, of his hold upon a large section of public opinion, possessed – to use current American terminology – a constituency of his own, as did no other politician. Planning its Election coverage, the Press Association assigned one reporter each to Wilson and to Heath; and two to Powell.

Yet there was no reason to suppose, the Tour affair apart, that the Election would be about race, or about foreign policy, or about the Common Market. There was every reason, instead, to suppose that this Election, like previous recent elections, would be about men rather than matters; that it would be between Heath and Wilson; and that the chief consideration each elector would give would be to what he considered to be his own interests and which of these two men would best serve them. Would the country choose the mixture as before? Or was it already time for a change? Did the electors feel better off under Labour than they had done under the Tories? What did they think the pound in their pocket was worth? Did they reckon their rising wage packets had kept up with the rising cost of living? For how much would it count, in their assessment, that Chancellor Jenkins had appeared to balance the books? Did they feel gloomy at the economy's lack of growth?

*   *   *

On Tuesday, 19th May, Heath travelled to Cambridge to fulfil a long-standing engagement to talk to dons and others. It had been thought that the previous day's announcement of the Election might have caused Heath to cancel the meeting, but with his characteristic courtesy in such matters he came along, and said to a gathering in the Combination Room at Peterhouse: 'We need a radical change in the style of government.' Lord Butler, being equally characteristic said '... Mr. Heath, the Leader of the Conservative Party,' and paused, while everyone expected to hear the routine 'and next Prime Minister of the country', but added instead 'for many years to come.' Heath may have suggested 'a radical change in the style of government'; not so Wilson, who the previous evening had had himself telerecorded in Downing Street garden, with birds singing in the early days of an incomparable summer which ran through blue skies and golden sunshine until Polling Day and well beyond. The Marplan Poll in *The Times* attributed a 2.7 per cent lead to Wilson, the same as an overall majority of 60. With any luck at all England might win the World Cup. Who, at a time like this, could possibly want a radical change in the style of government? What cloud was on the blue horizon?

There was, of course, one; and the Labour Government acted swiftly to dispel it. Callaghan, the

Home Secretary, issued an invitation on Wednesday, 20th May, to the Cricket Council to meet him at the Home Office on Thursday. Following the meeting, which was inconclusive, Callaghan made an official request of the Cricket Council that they call off the Tour. On 22nd May the Council held an emergency meeting at Lords, to consider Callaghan's request, made 'on grounds of broad public policy'. The Council 'were of the opinion that they had no alternative but to accede to the request'; and thus, to the great electoral advantage of the Labour Party, to the delight of the intimidators, to the relief of much of what still passed for the Establishment, and to the shame of the English political tradition and as an appalling hostage to the future, a campaign of blackmail through threat of violence was brought to its successful conclusion.

'Complacent, self-satisfied, tired and smug' Heath called Labour's attitude, speaking to Conservative candidates on 23rd May and declaring: 'as we have never in the past hesitated to carry through change wherever it was necessary to improve the conditions of the people, so now we are determined to make change our ally ... Our next government, building on the solid achievements of the past, will be a great reforming administration – reform for dealing with the tax system, bringing industrial relations up to date, improving the social services, providing greater choice, and extending opportunity. Our policies will be to give back to people their freedom to take on their own responsibilities and to develop to the full their own character.' This, as rhetoric, was all right so far as it went:

but there was nothing specific, nothing concrete. What tax reforms? What improved social services? What new choices and what extended opportunities? What freedom given back? Such questions were not asked at this innovatory meeting of candidates. There was, however, some questioning whether Mr. Powell could be asked to make a speech elucidating his policies 'which seem to have been misunderstood', to which Barber replied that Powell would be speaking in the campaign and that he, Powell, had always stuck to the Conservative Party's declared policy on immigration.

On 26th and 27th May the Conservative and Labour Party manifestos were successively published. They contained no surprises. The Tories refused to commit themselves to a Value Added Tax. On immigration the manifesto stated: 'There will be no further large scale permanent immigration. We will give assistance to Commonwealth immigrants who wish to return to their countries of origin, but we shall not tolerate any attempt to harass or compel them to go against their will.' The Labour manifesto contained no pledge on a Wealth Tax (which had been bruited around). Harold Wilson, introducing the manifesto, said that Labour had made Britain strong economically – one of the strongest economies in the world: 'We now want to go forward on the basis of that strength to make Britain a fairer, a greater place to live in.' It would not, I think, be unfair to regard both manifestos as relics of old traditions (as Wilson has since, privately, suggested). Apart from being the cause of editorial comment and newspaper and television summarizing and television discussion, they served no political or electoral purpose.

At this stage the Polls' descriptions was confused, the most recently taken – that of O.R.C. in the *Sunday Times* – suggesting that the Tories had regained the lead lost in April and could gain a working majority, while the other four suggested varying degrees of Labour success. It was the general feeling that in the week's television appearances Heath had done better than Wilson, who had been subjected to a particularly damaging series of viewers' questions, practically all of which suggested that he was untrustworthy, a liar, a breaker of pledges. But the campaign had barely begun, although the outline of each party's strategy was now known.

Heath was to conduct virtually all his Party's press conferences each morning at Central Office, and commute by chartered aircraft to the principal cities to deliver a formal speech each evening, returning in almost all cases to Albany for the night. Wilson, while also taking most of the press conferences, had determined to make fewer set speeches from platforms in the middle of cities and instead to travel throughout the country exhorting the faithful in their committee rooms, a technique he called 'meeting the people'.

The Liberal impact during the campaign, despite the elegance with which Lord Byers conducted the Liberal morning press conferences cannot be said to have at any point loomed large. What was to loom large, as was generally anticipated, was Enoch Powell.

On Saturday, 30th May, Powell published his Election Address. Not for him his Leader's emphasis on wage and price inflation. Claiming that recent immigration had brought the total to nearly two million, he wrote: 'In all our history nothing remotely similar has happened before. It carries a threat of division, violence and bloodshed of American dimensions, and adds a powerful weapon to the armoury of anarchy.' He advocated 'Halt all immigration now. This means ending automatic entry for wives and children.' His second plank was opposition to the Common Market: 'The Conservative Party is not yet committed to Britain entering the Common Market. I shall do my best to make sure we never do.' Heath, questioned on Powell, said in his constituency at Bexley 'Mr. Powell isn't saying anything that he hasn't said before.'

On Monday, 1st June, Heath and Wilson began their daily electoral routine as they were with minor modifications to continue until polling day. At the morning press conferences Wilson was altogether more relaxed than Heath. Labour's technical handling of the conferences was also superior, for usually Harry Nicholas, Secretary of the Party, acted as chairman and lightly controlled the questioning. Heath acted as his own chairman, which put him at a disadvantage whenever he wished to change a line of questioning. The Prime Minister was also usually accompanied on the platform by the Party's Head of Research, and if he wished to speak on a particular topic he would fetch along the appropriate Minister.

Heath, to begin with, spoke alone and sat alone. Special upholstered seats on either wing of the crescent-shaped seating arrangements for the press were reserved for Party officials, on one side being the publicists and speech-writers and opposite them on the other side the administrators. This conveyed the impression that they, as well as the press, were present principally to hear the word. Both Wilson and Heath would normally begin their press conferences with a short and prepared statement about this or that, intended chiefly for the television people. Also on that Monday the evening routine was established as it was largely to remain. Heath made his set-piece speech and Wilson made his tour of Committee Rooms. Heath said 'Taxes are far too high' and 'Here in Britain under Labour, the poor have become poorer. The pension today is worth less than it was four years ago. There are still three quarters of a million children living in families at or below the poverty line. We are spending less on rebuilding schools than we did four years ago. All this in spite of taxation. High taxation may be the friend of socialism, but it has become the enemy of real social progress. We say that taxes must be reduced. Socialism is no longer that radical reforming creed which it used to be. It is smug and without a soul. It is the poor who have been let down by Labour. These are the people we care about . . . These are the people the next Conservative Government is going to look after . . . It is out of prosperity, not out of high taxation, that we will find the means to pay for those less well off.'

Wilson, for his part was well enough pleased to have an egg thrown at him at Wealdstone and to assure party workers in Hampstead and Harrow and Ealing: 'There's a method in my madness. I want to get to a very large number of key constituencies. I want to meet the Party workers. We've got a summer election. It's great to have a summer election. It's going to be a happy fight, an exciting fight . . . I just want to wish you a happy campaign . . . I'll allow you ten minutes off your canvassing and addressing envelopes just so you can see me on T.V. at ten o'clock tonight . . . there is a lot of method in my madness. I said I wanted to go to committee rooms and on to the housing estates and that's what I'm going to do. It may be a different way of fighting the election but it's my way. There's nobody here so shameless that he'd come to these committee rooms tonight and not every other night for the rest of the campaign. There are a lot of fair weather friends coming back to the Party now . . . we like summer elections. Open air meetings. Factory gate meetings. The Tories can't have factory gate meetings, you know. Fine summer nights like this. It means on polling day we shall be on the job and it will still be light at ten o'clock at night, and if he's late getting home from work, there'll be time for tea and a clean-up a bit and go out and vote. Let's make it a happy election, an exciting election, a victorious election.'

Wilson was somewhat more serious in his pre-recorded T.V. broadcast; the statesman, sitting at his desk in Number Ten – a great stage prop –

saying earnestly: 'While we have been getting on with the job, they have been electioneering since 1966; running Britain down at home and abroad, exuberant only when Britain ran into economic difficulties, grudging even in their admissions when Britain was coming to success.' And Wilson also made the accusation he was to persist with: that the Tories were financially irresponsible, promising £1,500 millions of tax cuts and £1,000 millions of extra spending. 'No housewife' – there was a lot of electoral talk aimed at the housewife – 'is going to be taken in by this unscrupulous pretence that in this life you can get something for nothing.'

On Tuesday, 2nd June, *The Times* published a Marplan poll giving Labour a 3.7 per cent lead, and on Wednesday in the *Daily Express* the Harris poll gave a Labour lead of 5 per cent, equivalent to a majority of 70. The previous *Sunday Times,* O.R.C. poll with the Conservatives ahead by 2 points, looked more than ever an exceptional polling figure to which no one paid much attention. David Wood, however, reported in *The Times* 'The messages of the opinion polls continue to mystify many experienced Conservative politicians who, after intense activity in their constituencies during the past few days, insist that they have seen no evidence of the sudden transformation in the electoral balance.'

By now an issue of a kind had emerged, thanks to Panorama. Roy Jenkins had said: 'We've got one of the strongest balance of payments of any industrial country in the world at the present time.' On the same programme Lord Cromer, who had been

Governor of the Bank of England during the devaluation crisis, declared 'there's no question that any government that comes into power is going to find a very much more difficult financial situation than the new (Labour) government found in 1964'. Cromer was speaking as a Conservative; but Lord Kearton, chairman of Courtaulds and a Labour supporter, agreed with Cromer's judgment. The degree of authority to be attributed to Cromer and his interpretation of the figures, and the broader questions as to the strength or weakness of the British economy, began now to preoccupy many of the leading Tory campaigners, although on the Tuesday morning it was a journalist at Heath's press conference who first raised the Cromer–Kearton quotes.

By now public interest in the General Election was pretty high. Following George Brown on one day (2nd June) of his onerous whistle-stop electioneering, the size of the crowds that he drew, and the excitable and vehement opposition of the students wherever he came across them, demonstrated that there was no public apathy over the election, although at the same time it could hardly be claimed that there was much public debate of issues or even much public knowledge of what the issues were.

Heath was still dominating the Tory campaign. In a widely praised television broadcast on Tuesday night he appeared after the familiar television faces of Geoffrey Johnson Smith and Christopher Chataway, a process described in *The Guardian* thus: 'The effect of a commercial television advertisement leading up to the real product – Mr.

Heath.' On Wednesday morning Heath was in Wales and he held his press conference there. One consequence of this – and proof of the extent to which Heath was keeping the election campaign under his personal control – was that there was no Conservative Party press conference in London that morning at all. It was as if Heath felt, at this stage, that there was no one he was able completely to trust; or else he and his advisers felt it imperative that no one should be provided with the opportunity of a London press conference to steal any of the limelight that was going to Heath in Cardiff.

Also on Wednesday morning the advance copy of a speech was handed in to Transport House by a senior Cabinet Minister. It hung around for a while, attracting little attention. The Press Association picked up a copy and, in its customary fashion, issued an advance version embargoed not to appear until after delivery that evening. B.B.C. television armed a reporter with a copy of some of the words with instructions to make use of them that evening at the same time as, although a hundred miles distant from, their delivery. It was this speech which provoked a furore.

Speaking to a rally organized by Students for a Labour Victory at Central Hall, Westminster, the Minister of Technology, Mr. Wedgwood Benn, said: 'The flag of racialism which has been hoisted in Wolverhampton is beginning to look like the one that fluttered 25 years ago over Dachau and Belsen. If we do not speak up now against the filthy and obscene racialist propaganda still being issued under the imprint of Conservative Central Office, the forces of hatred will mark up their first success and mobilize for their next offensive.' Benn went on to say that the most evil feature of Mr. Powell's Conservatism was the hatred it was stirring up. This was playing on fear and fanning suspicion. When hate was released it got out of control quickly. 'Already Powell has spoken against the Irish. Anti-semitism is waiting to be exploited as Mosley exploited it before.' Mr. Heath, Benn continued, might be a good man, but his silence on what was one of the central questions of our time 'renders him quite unfit to lead our country in the seventies'.

Enoch Powell that evening was speaking to a great crowd in the Harry Mitchell Recreational Centre in Smethwick. I was at that meeting, having decided to spend a couple of days in the Birmingham area. Since the account I wrote for the *Evening Standard* itself became controversial, and provided evidence of the extreme hostility aroused among journalists by anything written that could be counted as favourable to Powell, I shall quote the relevant passages from it.

'A moment of undoubted dignity has occurred in this election. It may prove, too, to be a moment of historical significance. It came about in the most improbable circumstances. After the main speech, during the period allowed for questions, Mr. Larry Harris, declaring himself to be representing B.B.C. Television, repeatedly endeavoured to read out a prepared question.

'Unable to make himself heard, he was handed the microphone from the platform, whereupon he proceeded to read a lengthy extract from the attack made by Mr. Wedgwood Benn upon Mr. Enoch Powell, including references to racialism, to Dachau and Belsen. What had the speaker to say to that?

'The speaker rose and said: "For myself, in 1939 I voluntarily returned from Australia to this country, to serve as a private soldier against Germany and Nazism." There was an almost imperceptible pause. "I am the same man today."

'This was the moment of dignity. The speaker, Enoch Powell. The scene was the vast gymnasium of the Harry Mitchell Recreational Centre, Smethwick.

'The crowd, which had got impatient and angry during the long – and, many would think, improperly asked – B.B.C. question, now erupted with joyful and triumphant applause.

'There were at least 1,200 of them come to the gaunt hall in this dingy and decaying backwater of Birmingham and they weren't the well-heeled, and all but a handful of them were for Enoch.'

This article was the cause of a deputation of protest from editorial members of the *Evening Standard* to the Editor, Mr. Charles Wintour; and a degree of hostility towards me from journalist friends and acquaintances surprising in its intensity. I mention this since it corroborates the very general press dislike – and dislike is really too weak a word: distaste, even disgust, an almost pathological condition, would better describe the attitude of some very influential English and American journalists – of Enoch Powell.

That night after his own meeting in Birmingham the Prime Minister talked informally with several journalists. He was most relaxed and amiable, except when the subject of the Benn attack on Powell cropped up. Wilson made it clear that the speech, electorally, was very damaging to Labour, that he had not known of it in advance, and that, had he known of it he would have had the offending passages removed.

At their Press Conference on Friday, Wilson and Heath both chose to talk about doctors' pay, an issue which had been simmering away on the stove for over a week, occasionally stirred by one or the other, but largely, I think, a phony issue, in that I do not believe many electors were all that interested in doctors' pay (except the doctors). The Government, having first declared it would not announce its decision on the Kindersley Committee's report until after the Election, had changed its mind following meetings with the doctors' representatives in which Dr. Stevenson, secretary of the B.M.A., said that Mr. Crossman had argued that to give the whole award would imperil the economy. Heath made much of this alleged Crossman phrase, which Wilson said Crossman would deny having made, as indeed he did. Heath, despite considerable questioning on the subject, declined to say whether or not he would implement the full Kindersley terms. He, Heath, preferred to insist upon the Crossman phrase (whether made or not) that such an award would imperil the economy, being anxious to dispel the effect that Wilson and the weather might well be creating, that everything in the garden was lovely. The sun was still shining, the skies were still blue, the days were still golden.

At the week-end the polls, taken together, were steady, suggesting a Labour lead of over 4 per cent. Anthony King, professor of Government at Essex University, declared in the *Observer*, 'It will take a near miracle – or heavy abstentions – to stop Labour winning its third successive election victory next week.' On Saturday night Enoch Powell spoke in his constituency, devoting his attention to the economic situation. Elsewhere, eggs were thrown at the Tory chairman, Mr. Anthony Barber. The doctors threatened to refuse to sign sick notes from the following Wednesday. The Prime Minister said that the Government was making an all-out effort to stop the threatening newspaper strike.

On Monday, 8th June, at the beginning of the last full week of the campaign, Wilson decided he had better react to the growing Tory attack on the condition of the economy: 'We have reached a pretty pass,' the Prime Minister said at his Press Conference, 'when we have a major political party which is now in such straits that it has a vested interest in proclaiming an economic emergency in a country which is recognized throughout the world as having an economy of a strength such as we have not known in this country for many years past.' He was in his most chirpy, cheeky mood, supremely confident. 'When will the Conservative leader get it into his head that the £550 millions balance of payments we have now is a surplus, not a deficit? A surplus. A plus. Positive. Above the line. Black not red . . . If the Conservatives for their own electoral purposes want to write down Britain's achievements, no power on earth can stop them. I should have thought on these issues there is no group of men more qualified to sing small.'

Talks about the threatened newspaper strike broke down the next day. There were no national daily newspapers from Wednesday, 9th June, until Monday, 15th June, although the London evenings resumed on Saturday, 13th June and contracted editions of the Sunday papers appeared on Sunday, 14th June.

The strike – or, rather, the lack of national newspapers – now became the predominant factor in the campaign. Heath, asked whether he thought the absence of papers helped him or Wilson more, concluded, because of the difficulty of an Opposition putting its line across, 'Of course we're bound to suffer. We certainly suffer. I think we suffer more, yes.' Two or three of us had earlier discussed this question with the Prime Minister travelling down by train from Edinburgh to Newcastle. His view was that, despite the Tory loss through the general Tory inclination of the Press, the Government of the day lost most. Wilson's thesis was that a newspaper strike, unlike, say, car or dock or coal strikes, had an immediate effect on practically everybody. People are immediately irritated by the absence of their favourite newspaper at breakfast time or on the way to work. It is a strike which is immediately apparent, equivalent in this way to a television and radio strike, although in one way worse, for the amount of information carried in newspapers far exceeds that provided by radio and television. Not only is it an irritant. It is seen, like all irritating national events, by much of the public as a fault of the government of the day. Wilson himself made the most strenuous personal effort to have the strike called off, risking his own prestige in the process. My own feeling is that Wilson's view of the effects of the newspaper strike corresponds more closely to the truth than Heath's. Heath, before the strike, had managed to raise the question of the economy: was there a crisis or not? Heath and the Tories had constantly talked of the troubled state of industrial relations. Here, in the absence of newspapers, was proof on every empty breakfast table of that Tory proposition, if further proof were needed.

I do not think it was only reporters who felt that, in the absence of newspapers, an air of unreality had been introduced into the Election. The weather maintained its miraculous course; and England scraped into the quarter finals of the World Cup. Had the newspapers been published, there is little doubt what would have been their principal electoral themes: the increasing support shown for Labour in the polls; the increasing Tory attack on the economy; and Enoch Powell.

When the Sunday newspapers appeared on 14th June, the *Observer* and the *Sunday Times* both contained an analysis of the polls that had appeared or would have appeared and both reached almost identical conclusions and headlines. The *Observer* said, 'TODAY'S POLL VERDICT: 100-SEAT MAJORITY FOR WILSON?' The *Sunday Times* said 'LABOUR – BY 100?'. The Tory attack had been maintained throughout the week, but it had not seemed to yield results. By Saturday the interest therefore had switched to Powell again: and this time it was by Powell's deliberate choice. He made speeches on Thursday and on Saturday of a premeditated nature which created sensations.

On Thursday evening Powell spoke to his electors at the Woodfield Avenue School. This speech is printed in full elsewhere, but its essential points were, first, the suggestion that the people of the country were being misled on immigration figures, and second, his emotive assertion that 'There are at this moment parts of this town which have ceased to be part of England, except in the sense that they are situated within it geographically . . .'

Heath opened his Press Conference on the Friday morning saying: 'I want to talk to you first today about a matter of the utmost importance, which is that of immigration and race relations in Britain.' This was the first occasion in the campaign when he chose to speak on the subject rather than doing so in response to questioning. He said, in a prepared statement 'There must be the strictest possible control of immigration into this country. The Conservative Government in 1962, with Mr. Butler as Home Secretary, was the first Government to take action in the question of the immigration into Britain. We did so against the utmost hostility and bitterness from the Labour Party. We did so because we knew it was necessary. Our policy is that there should be strict control and that whether a person comes from the Commonwealth countries or non-Commonwealth countries they should only come into Britain if there is a specific job for them to do in a specific place and for a specific period. This of course does not mean that there are any limitations on their travel while they are here. But it is for a specific purpose to which [*sic*] they would be admitted. This means that under our policy, for a Commonwealth immigrant coming here there would no longer be automatic right of citizenship and right to settle here permanently. The second part of our policy is that those who are already here and are living permanently will be able to bring in their wives and children of school age if they wish,' meaning, of course, that any *new* immigrants would not necessarily be thus permitted. 'The next point of our policy is that those immigrants who wish to go home will be assisted by us to do so. And the last point is that everybody who is in this country will be treated in exactly the same way. There will be no discrimination of any kind. I have always set my face against this and I shall continue to do so.' The echo, unmistakably, is of Powell at Smethwick: 'I said that I set my face like flint against discrimination. It is still set like flint against discrimination.'

Heath referred to Powell's speech at Wolver-hampton the previous night: Heath's only *substantial* disagreement with Powell would seem to have been interpretative: 'I do not share Mr. Powell's opinion, as he would put it, about the number of immigrants who are wishing to return to their own countries ... But above all I do not share his pessimism about the future of race relations in this country, provided that proper policies are pursued.'

By now Heath, who earlier had seemed to err by his, at most, lukewarm criticism of Benn's attack on Powell, seemed to incur the press' accusation of Powellism – he, Heath, was being attacked for not having attacked, or disowned, or repudiated Powell. The presumption of the press at this point – very much certain individual members of the English and American press – was very marked, if by presumption one means engaging in direct political and electoral dispute as opposed to the natural function of a journalist at a press conference to inquire, clarify, elucidate.

By this stage, Benn had become a kind of justifiably provoked chap whereas Powell by meanly impugning the loyalty of 'civil servants who cannot answer back' (poor souls) had become an even greater villain than before. The American nature and origin of this entire line of questioning cannot be concealed. The interrogatory form, the presumption of guilt first in Powell, and by association, in Heath, was American, as was the accent of the principal prosecutor (Anthony Lewis, London correspondent of the *New York Times*). It did not seem to have occurred to this journalist that if anyone was employing McCarthy techniques at this point, he was among their number. 'Do you still hope to see Mr. Powell elected to Parliament? Is that still your hope?' Heath: 'Yes, he is a Conservative candidate and I want to see Conservative candidates elected to Parliament. At the same time there has never been any doubt about my views as far as Mr. Powell's policies on immigration are concerned.' 'Do you not feel that your reluctance to repudiate Mr. Powell leaves the Conservative Party open to criticism about attempting to pick up the Powellite vote?' Heath again rehearsed his dismissal of Powell from the Shadow Cabinet. The ignorance of some of his questioners was indicated by the next question: 'If Mr. Powell were chosen as deputy leader of the Party at the next Conference, would you resign?', and Heath was able to gain respite, saying amidst laughter 'The deputy leader of the Party is chosen by myself.'

On Friday, 12th June – Heath travelled to Manchester, to speak at the Free Trade Hall. The *Sunday Times* subsequently reported: 'It had gone well: supporters were gathering around with congratulations. "Good old Ted! . . . Well done, sir!" For once, Mr. Heath looked expansive, relaxed and happy. At this moment David Sells of the B.B.C. approached. His manner was apologetic, for he had unpleasant, even shattering, news to impart. Had Mr. Heath heard the latest National Opinion Polls result? It was 12.4 per cent. "For us, or against us?" asked Heath. "Against you, sir." "I'm afraid I can't make any comment," said Heath, and he went upstairs. His face had assumed, at once, the fixed artificial look that it had worn so many times during the week. The look of a man determined not to admit the appalling weight of evidence that says he has lost.

The news of that remarkable poll – with its suggestion that the Government could win a 180-seat majority – was naturally enough received differently in the Labour camp. Reaction there was summed up by a Cabinet Minister who said, reflectively, "I suppose that just about wraps it up." '

While Heath was thus cast down utterly, Wilson remained, naturally enough, as perky and indeed exuberant as ever. Also in Lancashire he was saying: 'When the Tories finally recognized that their mean Selsdon Park policies would be rejected by the British people they changed the strategy of their election campaign – policies out, stunts in . . . Any stunt that would get a headline. Stunts about the economy. Stunts about doctors' pay. And, phoniest of all, stunts about prices.' Back in London on Saturday morning the Prime Minister still, naturally enough, suffused with confidence, started talking about Northern Ireland, where what had happened was 'in fact the total refutation of the Selsdon law and order thesis'. Wilson did, however, envisage the possibility of defeat in a way: 'In the most extremely favourable assumption about the outcome of this election from the point of view of the Conservatives, they could not hope to win except by a narrow majority. There have been many who have said that with such a majority Mr. Heath would be a prisoner of the Powellites. So he would. But no less would he be a prisoner of the Paisleyites.' I do not myself believe that Wilson would thus have publicly discussed the possibility of a Tory victory were he not absolutely convinced that no such practical possibility existed.

Heath, at his Press Conference half an hour later, tried to pull things together: 'The Labour Party says that Britain is already strong. I say that it is sham sunshine – that Britain is not strong enough to deal with the problems of homelessness, poverty, deprivation, unemployment, increasing strikes, rising prices, and the problems of race relations in some of our great cities.' At this conference, it ought to be recorded, and for the third time during the campaign, Mr. Anthony Barber stuck his neck out, suggesting forcibly that, so far as he was concerned, after visiting Labour-held marginals the Tories had to win if they were to secure victory his experience did not at all add up to what the polls foretold. Nobody took much notice of him. Optimism of that kind was only to be expected of a party chairman.

In the evening Wilson, still in Lancashire, could not, or would not, change his line which obviously he felt to be correct, attacking his opponents by claiming 'The new Toryism is a return to the old Toryism, not just pre-1964 but pre-Macmillan, pre-Butler. Abrasive Toryism means not just wiping out the achievements of the past $5\frac{1}{2}$ years. Not just rejecting the standards on which we are insisting ... They are soft-pedalling now, but their Selsdon policy means that they would have to make deep and savage inroads into the social services.' Pleased with this, he repeated himself later on in his speech: 'Their Selsdon policies, however much they may be playing them down during this election, involve most deep and substantial inroads into the social services.'

And in Birmingham Powell spoke again, more 'emotively' than ever, adopting more than ever the prophetic tone: 'Britain at this moment is under attack.' He talked of the universities and of Northern Ireland, and of the mob. He talked again of 'the enemy'. It was the strangest of his series of speeches.

The general consensus on Monday was stated by *The Times*: 'With polling day only four days away, two new attacks from Enoch Powell have dealt the Tory leader's new-style election campaign a serious body blow. For Labour, it is an unsolicited gift.' A Gallup Poll in the vital marginal seats, published in the *Daily Telegraph*, gave Labour a lead of 7 per cent, although in the *Sunday Telegraph* the day previously another Gallup Poll (overall, not confined to the marginals) showed a reduction in the Labour lead to 2.5 per cent. The Monday daily newspapers, back after the strike, stressed the Tory split brought about by Powell. Wilson, campaigning on Sunday (traditionally Labour does so while the Conservatives and Liberals do not, lest they give offence to their church-going supporters), said 'If I have made a mistake in this election – and I am always willing to admit my mistakes – it is that I have spent too much time in Labour (marginal) constituencies and not enough in the Tory ones. I think I should have spent more time in the Tory ones'; meaning that he now felt that not only was he going to win the election, but win it with an increased majority.

On Monday morning Wilson did not mention Powell in his prepared statement: that his political instinct was not half so sure as *The Times* that Powell 'is an unmitigated liability to Mr. Heath'. Instead he talked about Northern Ireland and the Paisleyites. Heath talked of the increasing number of strikes, unemployment, rapidly rising prices, high taxation. Then he went on: 'Now I'd just like to say one thing before we come on to questions, and it is this – that over the week-end I made a statement; this has been widely reported on the press, radio and television. That statement was made after consultation with and with the full authority of the Shadow Cabinet. It obviously referred to the speeches of Mr. Powell but it also went much wider than that because it referred to the speeches of other people in this country including the speeches of the Leader of the Labour Party about Northern Ireland and Mr. Benn about other aspects in which he tried to smear the whole of the Conservative Party. That statement was absolutely clear. It reflects the position of the whole of the Shadow Cabinet. It reflects the position of the future Conservative Government and of the Conservative Party. I have nothing whatever to add to that – nothing whatever.'

The statement to which he referred and seemingly attached such importance, was not immediately available at the Tory Party headquarters nor did it figure largely in the morning newspapers. Central Office eventually produced copies of it, and it transpired that it was made after a request for a statement on Powell's Saturday speech, in response to a Press Association question made on Sunday. It was very short, reasserting Heath's claim to be advocating rational and humane policies, and declaring: 'We are a national party or we are nothing. My colleagues in the Shadow Cabinet and I will never use words or support actions which exploit or intensify divisions in our society and so damage the interests of the nation as a whole.' The principal consultation with the Shadow Cabinet to which Heath referred, and the securing of their assent, was by telephone. A questioner who attempted to mention Mr. Powell was cut off short by Heath: 'I've already said that I have nothing to add on that matter at all.'

That same Monday a trade deficit of £31 million for May was announced. Chancellor Roy Jenkins attributed £18.5 million of it to the purchase of two Jumbo jets. Shadow Chancellor Iain Macleod prophesised that June's unemployment figures would be the worst for any June since 1940. Several political friends of Powell standing for election spoke up in his support, including Victor Goodhew, Angus Maude, Sir Gerald Nabarro, Fergus Montgomery, Harold Soref, Richard Devonald-Lewis, John Holt, Major-General d'Avigdor-Goldsmid, Sir Richard Thompson, and Anthony Fell. Powell himself chose on Monday evening to deal with the, by now, comparatively uncontroversial Common Market issue.

On Tuesday morning Heath, flanked by Macleod and Joseph, declared that 'the country's economy is heading for a very serious position'. The Prime Minister said in Oldham that Heath was putting the pound at risk: and added 'Not in this generation has anyone been prepared to sell the country short to win votes.'

That Tuesday night I went into a working-class pub in Hammersmith to listen to Wilson deliver the final Party Political Broadcast of the election: the disinterest was almost total. People did not even turn to look or strive, momentarily, to listen. I was reminded of the remark of a London taxi-driver early in the campaign who had said to me: 'I picked up a fellow at the Carlton Club and I said to him, "the trouble with your lot is that you're a bunch of old women", and he said to me "Our Lord had many women followers".' Heath on Wednesday night said at Bexley: 'Tomorrow, in the privacy of the polling booth the women of Britain will tell Mr. Wilson what they've been dying to tell him for five years – they'll tell him they don't like it, and they'll tell him they're not going to have any more of it. They'll tell him they want a change.' That morning the polls had wobbled, although all still prophesied Labour victory.

But when Powell returned to his constituency on Tuesday he had delivered a different kind of speech which had ended: 'On Thursday your vote is about a Britain that, with all its faults and failings, is still free, and great because it is free. On Thursday your vote decides whether that freedom shall survive or not. You dare not entrust it to any government but a Conservative government.'

Harold Wilson, ending his campaign where he most likes to do it, at St. George's Hall, Liverpool, said: 'Pray God, the weather remains fine. There's only one party praying for rain, and it isn't us.'

The weather remained fine on polling day, and the Conservative Party won by an overall majority of 31.

4

The Opinion Polls and the General Election

by 'Poll Observer'

'Poll Observer' is a market researcher who, being a senior executive of a prominent public relations firm, writes anonymously.

The table below (which is based on data published in the *Financial Times* of 20th June, 1970) contains all the evidence:

THE RUN-UP TO POLLING DAY

Poll	Fieldwork dates	Labour lead %
	MAY	
Marplan	14–17	2.7
Gallup	13–17	7.0
N.O.P.	22–24	3.2
O.R.C.	20–24	2.0
Gallup	23–26	5.5
Marplan	28–31	3.7
N.O.P.	29–31	5.1
Harris	27–31	5.0
O.R.C.	28–31	*minus* 2.0
Gallup	31–June 4	5.5
	JUNE	
Harris	3–7	7.0
O.R.C.	4–6	2.0
N.O.P.	5–7	12.4
Gallup	7–11	2.5

Poll	Fieldwork dates	Labour lead
Harris	10–13	2.0
Marplan	11–14	8.7
N.O.P.	12–16	4.1
O.R.C.	13–17	minus 1.0
Gallup	14–16	7.0
Actual Result	18	minus 3.4

It is clear that the Opinion Polls failed to predict the result of the General Election. In 20 polls taken by five organizations during May and June, only two (both undertaken by O.R.C.) produced a Conservative lead (of 2 per cent and 1 per cent respectively). It is amusing to read the comments on this poll published in the *Sunday Times* for 7th June, 1970, as follows:

'This problem of sampling error, so vaguely understood by politicans and public, was last week weighing heavily on the mind of Humphrey Taylor, managing director of Opinion Research Centre. His poll, published last week in the *Sunday Times* and showing a 2 per cent Tory lead, was so patently out of line with the rest of the polls (including others of his own) that it was clearly a freak result. Lying sleeplessly in bed, he even composed a verse:

A poll every day
Causes dismay
When each has a different conclusion.
But when they agree
The critics shout, "see!
It's nothing but dirty collusion."

84

Opinion Research Centre have intensively re-checked the maverick poll but no biases have been found in its sample which could account for anything more than fractions of a per cent. ... About 20 polls will be published during the Election and last week Humphrey Taylor suspected his might have been the unlucky one.'

There are two types of explanation why this failure occurred. The first is that the opinion polls were technically deficient in some way or other and the second is that public opinion changed in such a way during the General Election that the polls were unable to cope with the problems involved.

The first type of explanation includes a large number of possible reasons for failure. The most discussed so far has certainly been differential turn-out. Only 72 per cent of the electorate voted and Louis Harris has said that this low turn-out (presumably particularly low amongst Labour supporters) was one big reason why his opinion polls went wrong. In his own words:

'One key to this election which the Harris Poll did not utilize as fully as it might was turn-out. ... Our poll showed a six point difference in voting intentions amongst electors of each main party. ... Had we fully applied this turn-out differential, the final Harris Poll would have been a two point Tory rather than Labour lead.'

Hoinville and Jowell (*New Society* 2nd July, 1970) dismiss this explanation (as have Anthony

King and Marplan on other occasions). In their own words:

> 'An analysis of the size of swing to Conservatives in individual constituencies shows no real correlation between swing and *fall* in turn-out (i.e. the drop in percentage poll between 1966 and 1970). We carried out a "rank correlation test" on the results of the first 417 declared seats, between the drop in turn-out and the size of the swing to the Conservatives. The correlation was almost nil (to be precise it was 0.07). Nor was there any greater correlation between swing and the 1970 turn-out as such – i.e. with the constituencies rated simply according to their percentage poll independently of how turn-out was last time. The evidence does not support any relationship between size of swing and turn-out.'

This argument is not entirely convincing. For example, if Labour voters failed to vote in exactly similar proportions in all constituencies, then there would be no positive correlation between swing and fall in turn-out – yet at some point the Conservatives would certainly win the Election. How important differential turn-out was in producing the discrepancy between the polls and the Election result remains an unanswered question.

A number of other explanations have been suggested. It has been said that the sample sizes were much too small, that the sample designs were inadequate, that people were reluctant to say they would vote Conservative for fear of being thought a racialist by the interviewer, that not enough money and time had been invested by the polling organizations in developing more sophisticated ways of measuring the depth of feeling on an issue. This last point has considerable validity and indeed the difference between the findings of the various polling organizations was evidence – if it had been looked at in this way – that this was not going to be an easy election for the forecaster using traditional methods. William Gregory, a very experienced pollster, writing in the *New Statesman* (26th June, 1970) had this to say:

'Are their methods out of date? The polling errors have to be set in the context of the amazing fluctuations revealed between elections both in poll results and in by-election results. On the evidence of the polls – there is no other – the parties have lost much of their identification with class and sectional interests: people have moved away from the predispositions induced by birth and circumstance; emancipation increases cross-voting, the wife in difference to her husband, children in difference to their parents; mass media communicate with unprecedented speed and persuasion to people who formerly lived in small closed circles. All this and much else suggests that questions which worked well enough in a stable, unexposed society are no longer satisfactory.

'A main culprit, though by no means the only one, may well be the "How will you vote?" type of question. Reinforced by organizational insistence to interviewers that "don't know" is an unacceptable answer, the hallmark of unsatisfactory interviewing, it labels too many who should be recorded as "Undecided" ... Meteorology has improved as a science by multiplying the numbers and kinds of observations and by greater scope and sophistication in the analysis. The polls must follow this example.'

The other type of explanation for the failure of the Opinion Polls in the 1970 Election is that the Opinion Polls were not wrong but in a sense simply out-of-date. That is to say, they were measuring something that was changing quickly and they failed to be sufficiently up-to-date with their measurements. This explanation has been put forward by several of the polling organizations, notably Gallup and Louis Harris, both of whom have stated that in future they intend to continue carrying out their surveys right up to eve of Election Day. Gallup have undertaken some research since the Election, the results of which were reported in the *Daily Telegraph* for July 10th, 1970. These results show that the Conservatives won the General Election in the last few days of the campaign. In Gallup's own words:

'People continued to change their minds right up to polling day, after Gallup had stopped measuring the country's voting intentions. After 18th June Gallup went back to some of the people interviewed in their final poll to see how and why they had changed.

'The movement from Labour indicated by

88

these recalls confirms Gallup's view that their last poll, showing Labour ahead, was correct when the original interviews were conducted – between 14th and 16th June. The changes occurred in the two days between the end of fieldwork and publication of 18th June . . .

'For their recall survey, Gallup re-interviewed 684 people, concentrating on the 387 people who in the final pre-election poll had said they would vote Labour. This group showed the biggest change.

'Only 77 per cent voted Labour, most of the rest did not vote, but seven per cent voted Conservative. Although Conservative supporters also showed less than 100 per cent loyalty, the net movement was from Labour to Conservative.

'Of the 26 people who switched from Labour to Conservative, 10 said the Conservative party had better policies, four thought it was time to change, two cited Labour's broken promises and the economy, two mentioned the local candidate and only one said Mr. Enoch Powell.'

This argument is not accepted by everyone. Lord Poole, for example, has said recently that there was no swing in public opinion during the General Election. William Gregory seems to agree in the sense that he has pointed out that the evidence casting most doubt on the last-minute switch explanation is provided by the success of the polls in individual constituencies. The two polls with the largest error, says Gregory, had notable local success, Gallup in Orpington and Marplan in a number of Midland constituencies. Hoinville and Jowell also do not believe that there was a massive swing to the Conservatives in the final week. They say:

'This seems equally implausible. Some one and a half million voters would have needed to change their minds during the last few days to account for the discrepancy between, for example, the *Sunday Times* index of 7th June (predicting a Labour victory by 60 seats) and actual voting behaviour. And this means changes of mind, not late deciders.

If this had occurred, and had determined the result of the election, it would have been a momentous political feat. It is true that the theory of a last-minute volte-face on the part of some one and a half million electors – pretty well uniformly distributed over the country – cannot actually be exploded. Yet it seems far-fetched.'

It is important to recognize that we do not have – and cannot have – any evidence on whether people in general changed or did not change their voting intentions during the General Election. We can, with some difficulty, try to find out whether people interviewed in surveys changed their minds. But all that this tells us is that people interviewed in surveys – and thereby forced to decide on their voting intentions – changed or did not change their minds. It can tell us nothing about the 99 per cent of electors who were not interviewed. This means that Hoinville and Jowell are quite wrong to dismiss the 'swing' argument in the way they do.

The most likely explanation seems to be that suggested in passing by Gregory and Lovell (in *Advertiser's Weekly* 26th July, 1970). Politics are increasingly unreal to a large number of people, particularly the young. Class and educational backgrounds are increasingly unconnected with political affiliations. As a result, a considerable number of people in this Election were undecided (and that is too strong a word in itself) right up to the end of the campaign. They were looking for a sign to help them decide. In this sense, there was no swing in opinion because that implies a change in decision-making from one side to the other: there was more a hardening of opinion than a switch in voting intentions.

If this explanation is true (and evidence for it is totally lacking), then why did opinion harden in favour of the Conservatives? There are several possible explanations: the publication of bad trade figures, England's defeat in the World Cup on the Sunday before the Election Day, the emergence of the racial issue through Enoch Powell's speeches, the soft-sell nature of the campaign waged by the Labour party. No one knows whether any or none of these explanations is particularly important; but on the evidence available and using common-sense judgment it seems reasonable to say that the World Cup defeat and Enoch Powell were probably the more important influences in helping more people than the Opinion Polls predicted – a million or so of them – to vote Conservative on 18th June, 1970. *See 'STOP PRESS' on page 125.*

5

Enoch Powell's Campaign Speeches

Rt. Hon. J. Enoch Powell, M.B.E., M.P.

BALANCE OF PAYMENTS AND PRICES
Wolverhampton, Saturday, 6th June, 1970

I am far from thinking that at this election the principal issues for many people are economic. Nevertheless, over the country as a whole it may well be the electorate's judgment on two economic matters which determines the outcome of the General Election. Those two matters are the balance of payments and the cost of living. On both the public has been subjected during the past four or five years to a continuous process of indoctrination. On the one hand, they have been hypnotized into believing that it was an almost miraculous achievement of the Government to 'get the balance of payments right', and that an admiring electorate ought to be humbly grateful. On the other hand, they have been hypnotized into believing that the spiral of rising prices and rising wages is no fault at all of the Government but is due to the misbehaviour of people themselves, from which the Government has vainly but gallantly attempted to save them.

Both beliefs are entirely unfounded; both beliefs

are highly dangerous. The truth is that no thanks at all are owed the Government for the surplus on our balance of payments, but that the rise in our cost of living is entirely their handiwork and their fault.

Balance of payments is really devastatingly simple: it depends upon the level of the exchange rate. If that is too high, then a country has a deficit. If it is too low, the same country has a surplus. There is no way out of this. One could say of the balance of payments, what Lord Melbourne is supposed to have said of the Garter, that 'there is no damn merit about it'.

Until the end of 1967 the £ sterling was overvalued, and more and more severely overvalued. Consequently, whatever efforts we made, we were bound to have a deficit. Since the end of 1967 or shortly afterwards, the £ has been undervalued. Consequently we have been basking in the sunshine of a large surplus. If the rate had not been changed in 1967, we should be in deficit still – provided other countries had not got tired of lending us money in order to keep us there.

An increasing number of people are realizing that it is idiotic to try to keep the exchange rate fixed, and therefore be periodically obliged to devalue or revalue, whereas if the exchange rate were free to move upwards and downwards, like any other price, it would keep payments automatically in balance with no trouble to anybody. I have been saying this for a long time. Mr. Maudling has been saying it for longer still. True, he got his knuckles rapped for his pains; but those of us who get our knuckles rapped are not always wrong. Be that as it may, however – whether we float the pound, as the Canadians have just floated their dollar, or whether we go on with the old game of fixed exchange rates – the Government can claim not a scrap of credit for Britain's deficit turning into surplus. All their pulling and pushing, all their credit squeezes and their high interest rates, all their swingeing taxation and their attempts to control prices and wages – all these, like the flowers that bloom in the spring tra-la, have nothing to do with the case. The surplus on our balance of payments is the purely automatic and inevitable result of the adjustment of our exchange rate – nothing more, nothing less.

Yet it is on the strength of this bogus achievement that the Government would have us forget or forgive all that has gone before, and come back for more of it, like the whipped hound which turns to kiss the rod.

If there are any doubters, let them just recall what happened last autumn when the German mark was revalued, as the £ had been devalued. All of a sudden, that wonderful surplus for which we had so long envied the Germans, for which they had been held up to our admiration as incomparably enterprising, energetic, thrifty, hard-working, disappeared practically overnight and was replaced by a deficit which they were fain to meet by borrowing – yes, by borrowing. Nothing had changed, nothing in the German character, nothing in the policy of the German government, nothing – except the exchange rate itself. Likewise in Britain nothing has changed, neither the British character nor the policy of the British Government – only the exchange rate itself. So let us hear no more of the fraudulent claim of the Government upon our gratitude for having 'got the balance of payments right'.

It is the opposite way round with the cost of living. True, not even the Government can dispute that it has risen faster since they were in office than since they were in office before, and at a rate which accelerated as time has gone by. This they do not attempt to deny. This they cannot deny. Instead, they would have us believe that they are not to blame, but are the innocent victims of the perversity of the British people who persist in charging and paying higher prices and in demanding and receiving higher wages. With that streak of masochism which is part of the British character, we have positively revelled in lapping up this falsehood. The truth is that the rise in the cost of living is due neither to British trade unions, nor to British industry, nor to the British economy; it is due wholly and solely to the British Government.

I have looked up a speech which I made in February 1965, three or four months after the Socialists came into office. The then Chancellor of the Exchequer had declared that under this Government public expenditure was going to rise at the planned rate, no matter whether the national income as a whole rose faster or slower. From that moment it was a virtual certainty, and I predicted it, that the cost of living would get out of hand. Here again the working of cause and effect is devastatingly simple. When the expenditure of the Government is rising faster than the national income, it is odds-on that what it spends will exceed what taxation brings in and that the public will not be willing to lend it sufficient savings to fill the gap. There can only be one result: the Government will create sufficient extra money to meet its expenditure. This is what happened, and happened on an increasing and eventually gigantic scale, from 1965 to 1968. While production lagged and the national income rose at a snail's pace, public expenditure soared upwards. As a result, vast quantities of additional money were pumped into the economy. If trade unions had never been invented and if the population had consisted of Benedictine monks, the consequence would still have been, inevitably and automatically, the rise in prices (including wages) which we have experienced.

The one achievement on which the Government need fear no challenge is that of manufacturing money. It is the money they have manufactured to meet their own exorbitant expenditure that has devalued the pound in everyone else's pocket. May be, the trade unions have much else to answer for; certainly, the legal framework of industrial relations and trade unionism cries aloud for reform. May be, (why should we dispute it?) our production could be more efficient and our commerce more competitive. But the one fault that cannot be laid to either of these quarters is the rise in the cost of living. Only an increase in money could cause all prices and all wages to rise as they have done. Only the Government and the Government's expenditure could cause the increase in money.

96

The true verdict on the Government's record runs therefore as follows. Surplus on the balance of payments: *innocent*. Rise in the cost of living: *guilty*.

IMMIGRATION

Wolverhampton, Thursday, 11th June, 1970

I have not so far in any speech in this election campaign referred to Commonwealth immigration into the United Kingdom and its consequences, present or prospective. It is in fact a subject on which I speak rarely – three or four times a year at most – and with greater deliberation and care than upon any other. Nevertheless, I have not concealed my belief that this subject exceeds all others in its importance for the future not only of this town and other areas already directly affected, but of the entire nation. I thought it right to say so plainly in my election address, especially as the policies of the opposing parties in regard to it differ sufficiently to offer the electorate a real and substantial choice. It would be absurd therefore if I were to refrain from speaking about this subject here, to my own electorate, before the election comes to an end.

I do not intend tonight to attempt a general survey of the problem. My object is to concentrate upon a few major points which are in danger of being ignored or suppressed.

The first, which cannot be emphasized too often, is that of number. The scale of Commonwealth immigration into this country in the last twenty years – apart altogether from the nature of that immigration – is already in point of numbers out of all comparison greater than anything these islands have ever experienced before in a thousand years of their history. People who talk in this context about the immigration of one or two hundred thousand Jews from Europe before World War I or of the Huguenots from France only reveal that they have no conception of the facts.

What I have said in the last two or three years about the numbers of Commonwealth immigrants and their increase has been treated over and over again with derision and with that abusive obloquy which is intended to obviate the need for rational discussion. But as the facts have at last, grudgingly and partially, been revealed, it has turned out that I was right and my traducers were wrong. Indeed, the figures which have become known in the last year, or year and a half, have in every case proved to be higher than I myself would have guessed. If I have been guilty on this score, it is *under*statement that has been my offence. On this subject, so vital to their future, the people of this country have been misled, cruelly and persistently, till one begins to wonder if the Foreign Office was the only department of state into which enemies of this country were infiltrated.

Earlier this year we learnt that the Government had been grossly underestimating the size of the annual addition to the Commonwealth immigrant population by natural increase. After making all conceivable allowances – some of them quite ludicrous – I showed that the true increase would still be almost 60 per cent greater than the Government had estimated. On the basis of any reasonable assumptions (instead of extravagantly low ones) the true excess is about 100 per cent. This can only mean that the size of the present immigrant population, or its birth rate, or the two combined, are twice what the Government had assured us.

The immigrant population is now certainly nearer 2 million than the $1\frac{1}{4}$ million which the Government allege. Those who talk about 'only 2 per cent' of the population of England and Wales are misled, however innocently; 4 per cent is already nearer the mark.

Most people have no conception how fast that percentage is growing. Last year there was almost the same increase in the white and in the coloured population of this country. It is not enough to look at the proportion of coloured births to total births. You have also to look at the large net *emi*gration of white residents and the large net *imm*igration of coloured residents. When these are taken into account, we find that between 90,000 and 100,000 a year net is being added *on each side*. At that rate the proportion between the two is altering very rapidly.

I know it is dinned into us that net Commonwealth immigration is rapidly falling; but this, like so much else that is fed to the British people by this Government, is misleading. The fact is that net immigration in 1969 was back again to practically the same figure as in 1966, after having been higher – much higher – in the two intervening years, 1967 and 1968. When we are told that the first quarter of 1970 was lower again, that too is misleading. The fall in 1969 only took place in the second half of the year, when the delay took effect which was imposed by the new requirement of entry certificates. In fact, the first quarter of 1969 was actually running above previous levels. No doubt, net Commonwealth immigration will gradually fall. On the other hand, it is not denied that for a time the births will go on rising; and if this Government were to remain in office after the election, I would not care to answer for the effect on the numbers of our own people emigrating.

However, as we in Wolverhampton well know, the total figures, though much larger and growing much faster than people had been led to believe, convey no impression of the reality, when divided into the entire population of England and Wales so as to yield an overall percentage. The reality is what we see emerging before our eyes in the transformation of this and other towns and cities, including the inner part of the Metropolis itself. When I referred, two years and more ago, to 'whole areas, towns and parts of towns across England being occupied by different sections of the immigrant and immigrant-descended population', the prediction was derided and denounced. The facts which have become known since then have proved it true. I have demonstrated that, even after making every concession, however improbable, however unreal, a fifth or a quarter of such towns and cities as Wolverhampton, Birmingham and Inner London will in course of time consist of the

Commonwealth immigrants and their descendants. There has been no attempt at refutation. No refutation is possible. Those who mocked two years ago have taken refuge either in silence or in abuse. Once again, I have erred – perhaps all too much – on the side of understatement: the rational probability is much larger. Indeed, what I said is already ceasing to be prediction and becoming current fact. There are at this moment parts of this town which have ceased to be part of England, except in the sense that they are situated within it geographically.

So – number is of the essence, and geographical concentration is of the essence, and each multiplies the effect of the other. Now I turn to the consequences of number and of concentration. These neither I nor anyone else can prove in advance; but if, when the consequences occur, it would be too late to reverse them, it is the politician's duty to form and to declare his judgment of them in time, so that, if possible, they may be averted or modified. I declare, then, that in my judgment, based upon what knowledge I have of human nature and upon what observation I have made of events in the world, the prospective growth in this country of the Commonwealth immigrant and immigrant-descended population will result in civil strife of appalling dimensions, and that institutions and laws, let alone exhortations, will be powerless to prevent it. On the other hand, it is not in my judgment yet too late to prevent or greatly reduce those consequences – namely, by a great reduction of the prospective number.

Like any other man, I can be mistaken; I can be mistaken either about the consequences or, if I am not mistaken about those, then I can be mistaken about the possibility of averting them. What is certain is that whatever the consequences are, my words could not cause them and my silence could not avert them. What is also certain is that anyone bearing the responsibility of a Member of Parliament who judged as I do but held his peace, would be guilty of a crime against his country and his fellow men. There are some so foolish as to imagine, or so malevolent as to pretend, that those who think they foresee danger or disaster, therefore desire it. One might as well accuse a man who warned against a rearming enemy of desiring the war he hoped to avert.

That nation will be ill counselled which allows its statesmen to predict only what it is pleasant to hear.

The reduction of prospective numbers depends upon two courses of action. One is the cessation of further immigration. On this I find nothing to alter in what I said over two years ago: 'We must be mad, literally mad, as a nation to be permitting the annual inflow of some 50,000, who are for the most part the material of the future growth of the immigrant-descended population.' However, I would be deceiving you if I allowed you to suppose that in my opinion the cessation of further immigration would sufficiently reduce prospective numbers to modify at all appreciably the consequences I foresee. I wish I could think so; but I cannot. Therefore it follows that a major re-emigration or repatriation is essential if it is possible. The Conservative Party has adopted the policy of assisting the repatriation and resettlement of all who wish to avail themselves of the offer, without limitation of numbers. My own judgment is that the numbers, if this policy is adopted promptly and wholeheartedly, could be decisive; and I am fortified in this by the fact that my estimate of half was reached by, among others, one of the most brilliant and impartial judicial minds in the country, Lord Radcliffe's. To the doubters I say: since when has it been an argument against adopting measures to combat a danger, to say that they might not, or might not fully, succeed?

The last point that I wish to emphasize is one which certainly does not need emphasizing to the people of this town and ought not to need emphasizing to any person of intelligence and impartiality. It is that to speak and act as I have done implies no ill will towards Commonwealth immigrants or any section of them, but much the contrary. Like the overwhelming majority of my fellow countrymen, I hold no man inferior because he is of different origin. As the Member during twenty years for a constituency which has had a higher influx of Commonwealth immigrants, and for longer, than almost any other, I have invariably given the same service and shown the same good will to my immigrant constituents as to the rest. They have the same claim upon me, and it has been equally discharged; and many there are who can testify to that. And so it shall always be.

But I owe to them, along with the rest, another

and a higher duty. If my judgment of the dangers of the future is right, then the immigrants and their descendants have, if possible, even more to gain than the rest of us from those dangers being averted; for the outcome which I believe is portended would be at least as disastrous for the newcomers as for the indigenous inhabitants. What I have said, I have said in the interest of all.

THE ENEMY WITHIN

Northfield, Birmingham, Saturday, 13th June, 1970

Britain at this moment is under attack. It is not surprising if many people still find that difficult to realize. A nation like our own, which has twice in this century had to defend itself by desperate sacrifice against an external enemy, instinctively continues to expect that danger will take the same form in the future. When we think of an enemy, we still visualize him in the shape of armoured divisions, or squadrons of aircraft, or packs of submarines. But a nation's existence is not always threatened in the same way. The future of Britain is as much at risk now as in the years when Imperial Germany was building dreadnoughts, or Nazism rearming. Indeed the danger is greater today, just because the enemy is invisible or disguised, so that his preparations and advances go on hardly observed. When Czechoslovakia was dismembered or Austria annexed or Poland invaded, at least one could see that a shift of power had taken place; but in the last three years events every whit as pregnant with peril have given no such physical signal.

As we prepare to elect a new Parliament, the menace is growing, as such dangers do, at an accelerating pace. Other nations before now have remained blind and supine before a rising danger from within until it was too late for them to save themselves. If we are to escape the same fate, it is high time we opened our eyes; for the first condition of self-defence is to see what it is we have to fear.

I assert, then, that this country is today under attack by forces which aim at the actual destruction of our nation and society as we know or can imagine them. The same forces are at work in other western countries too. Indeed, in some other countries they are more advanced than in this country. However, just as it is no consolation to be told by the Prime Minister that other nations have inflation too, so here there is no salvation in common peril. A plague is not less deadly because it is not confined to a single country. Nevertheless, it is useful to be able to register in terms of other countries as well as our own the advances which the enemy has made in the last three, or at most four, years. Let me remind you of them.

In those three or four years we have seen the universities of America being destroyed. Those institutions are now not merely the permanent scene of violence and disorder, but they only exist and are administered upon terms dictated by the enemy; they have passed out of the control of authority. In the same period we have seen the same enemy in his student manifestation not only terrorize one European city after another, but bring down one of the strongest European governments. In this country we have seen the institutions of learning systematically threatened, browbeaten and held up to ridicule by the organizers of disorder.

So much for the universities; but civil government itself has been made to tremble by the mob – in its modern form, the demonstration. The actual policy and administration of the United States has been altered, and altered again, not by the votes of the electors or the decisions of Congress, but by the fact or the fear of crowd behaviour. Nor need we go abroad for our examples. We have seen in this country in the last few weeks how the menace of organized disorder could threaten the morale of the police and wield the authority of the state itself not in favour of the peaceable citizen but against him. When the *Prince of Wales* and the *Repulse* disappeared beneath the waters of the Gulf of Siam, at least we knew that Britain had suffered a defeat. We suffered no less decisive a defeat when Britain's Home Secretary surrendered the rule of law in order to buy off demonstrations; but do we know that it was a defeat, or are people so foolish as to suppose that such an event is the end of a humiliating story, and not rather the beginning?

A considerable portion of the British Army is at this moment on active service in a province of the United Kingdom. But it is not in Northern Ireland to put down rebellion, nor is it there to repel invasion, though both those things may be woven into the future pattern of events. It is there because disorder, deliberately fomented for its own sake as an instrument of power, had come within an ace of destroying the authority of the civil government, and because the prospect of that authority being easily recovered is not foreseen. That the enemy has utilized the materials of religious division is almost as fortuitous as that a mob should use missiles from a near-by building site.

Nor is religious difference the only material that can be made to serve this purpose. On this side of St. George's Channel combustible material of another kind has been accumulated for years, and not without deliberate intention in some quarters. The exploitation of what is called 'race' is a common factor which links the operations of the enemy on several different fronts. In the last three or four years we have seen one city after another in the United States engulfed in fire and fighting, as the material for strife provided by the influx of Negroes into the Northern States, and their increase there, was flung into the furnace of anarchy. 'Race' is billed to play a major, perhaps a decisive, part in the battle of Britain, whose enemies must have been unable to believe their good fortune as they watched the numbers of West Indians, Africans, and Asians concentrated in her major cities mount towards the two million mark, and no diminution of the increase yet in sight.

One of the most dangerous characteristics of any aggressor is the ability to make his intended victim underestimate his power. This characteristic the present enemy possesses to a high degree. 'Fortunately,' people are heard saying, 'it is only a small minority which is involved.' There could be no greater ineptitude. In any event, all revolutions are made by minorities, and usually by small minorities. But those who talk in this way have not grasped the force and novelty of the new psychological weaponry with which they are being attacked. It is as if someone were to dismiss the discovery of the nuclear weapon with the offhand observation that 'the bomb is only a very small one'. It is small, yes, but it is nuclear.

The power of the minority, which, though still only in its infancy, we have watched being exerted here and elsewhere during the last few years, derives from its hold over men's minds. The majority are rendered passive and helpless by a devilishly simple, yet devilishly subtle, technique. This is to assert manifest absurdities as if they were self-evident truths. By dint of repetition of the absurdities, echoed, re-echoed and amplified by all the organs of communication, the majority are reduced to a condition in which they finally mistrust their own senses and their own reason, and surrender their will to the manipulator. In all war the objective is to break the opponent's will. Our danger is that the enemy has mastered the art of establishing a moral ascendancy over his victims and destroying their good conscience.

People observing the advance of anarchy call for more police, more punishment, more force. These may indeed be necessary; but in themselves they are impotent – in fact, they can become additional weapons in the enemy's armoury – unless the battle is simultaneously fought and won in the moral sphere. The decisive act is to put sense and nonsense, truth and absurdity, back into their right places; and that act is already so difficult that conventional wisdom and polite society have come to regard it as impossible. Have you ever wondered, perhaps, why opinions which the majority of people quite naturally hold are, if anyone dares express them publicly, denounced as 'controversial', 'extremist', 'explosive', 'disgraceful', and overwhelmed with a violence and venom quite unknown to debate on mere political issues? It is because the whole power of the aggressor depends upon preventing people from seeing what is happening and from saying what they see.

The most perfect, and the most dangerous, example of this process is the subject miscalled, and deliberately miscalled, 'race'. The people of this country are told that they must feel neither alarm nor objection to a West Indian, African and Asian population which will rise to several millions being introduced into this country. If they do, they are 'prejudiced', 'racialist', 'unchristian' and 'failing to show an example to the rest of the world'. A current situation, and a future prospect, which only a few years ago would have appeared to everyone not merely intolerable but frankly incredible, has to be represented as if welcomed by all rational and right-thinking people. The public are literally made to say that black is white. Newspapers like the *Sunday Times* denounce it as 'spouting the fantasies of racial purity' to say that a child born of English parents in Peking is not Chinese but English, or that a child born of Indian parents in Birmingham is not English but Indian. It is even heresy to assert the plain fact that the English are a white nation. Whether those who take part know it or not, this process of brainwashing by repetition of manifest absurdities is a sinister and deadly weapon. In the end, it renders the majority, who are marked down to be the victims of violence, or revolution, or tyranny, incapable of self-defence by depriving them of their wits and convincing them that what they thought was right is wrong. The process has already gone perilously far, when political parties at a general election dare not discuss a subject which results from and depends on political action and which for millions of electors transcends all others in importance; or when party leaders can be mesmerized into accepting from the enemy the slogans of 'racialist' and 'unchristian' and applying them to lifelong political colleagues.

But this is only one, if the most glaring, example; for there is no end to the use of absurdity, like obscenity, as a weapon for brain-smashing.

In the universities, we are told that the education and the discipline ought to be determined by the students, and that the representatives of the students ought effectively to manage the institutions. This is nonsense – manifest, arrant nonsense; but it is nonsense which it is already obligatory for academics and journalists, politicians and parties, to accept and mouth, upon pain of verbal denunciation and physical duress.

We are told that the economic achievement of the Western countries has been at the expense of the rest of the world and has impoverished them, so that what are called the 'developed' countries owe a duty to hand over tax-produced 'aid' to the governments of the undeveloped countries. It is nonsense – manifest, arrant nonsense, but it is nonsense with which the people of the Western countries, clergy and laity – but clergy especially – have been so deluged and saturated that in the end they feel ashamed of what the brains and energy of Western mankind have done, and sink on their knees to apologize for being civilized and ask to be insulted and humiliated.

Then there is the 'civil rights' nonsense. In Ulster we are told that the deliberate destruction by fire and riot of areas of ordinary property is due to dissatisfaction over allocation of council houses and opportunities for employment. It is nonsense – manifest, arrant nonsense; but that has not prevented the Parliament and government of the United Kingdom from undermining the morale of civil government in Northern Ireland by imputing to it the blame for anarchy and violence.

Most cynically of all, we are told, and told by bishops forsooth, that communist countries are the upholders of human rights and guardians of individual liberty, but that large numbers of people in this country would be outraged by the spectacle of cricket matches being played here against South Africans. It is nonsense – manifest, arrant nonsense; but that did not prevent a British Prime Minister and a British Home Secretary from adopting it as acknowledged fact.

It may have been a happy chance that this particular triumph of organized disorder and anarchist brainwashing coincided with the commencement of this General Election campaign. For many people it lifted a corner of the veil; for the first time, they caught a glimpse of the enemy and his power. If so, it was timely. That power lies in what we are made to say (or not say), and thus ultimately made to think (or not think). That power can only be broken by plain truth and commonsense, and the will to assert it loud and clear, whoever denies, whoever jeers, whoever demonstrates. Without that, there is no escape from the closing trap; no victory over those who hate Britain and wish to destroy it. Next week the people have it in their hands, perhaps for the last time, to elect men who will dare to speak what they themselves know to be the truth.

COMMON MARKET

Tamworth, Staffs, Monday, 15th June, 1970

For many electors this is a most frustrating General Election. They find, in a way that perhaps has never happened before, that they cannot use their vote to express their wishes on what seem to them the most important political questions. They can vote as between socialism and private enterprise, more nationalization or less, and all the rest of that ilk; but on decisions, national decisions, which could be more important still, the electors find themselves confronted with a virtual unanimity between the official parties and often between the respective candidates in their own constituencies.

The party system seems no longer to do its work of offering a choice between policies, and it is not surprising to hear so many demanding that the parliamentary system itself should be short-circuited, and the people offered the direct opportunity to say Yes or No by referendum.

Of all the subjects on which this demand is heard, and this frustration felt, the most widespread is that of the Common Market, and not surprisingly, for the question of joining the Common Market is the most fundamental of all. It is the question not merely what *sort* of a nation are we to be, but *what* nation are we to be?

I say at once that I am no supporter of a referendum, least of all on this sort of subject. Out of many reasons I mention only two. First, it is inconsistent with the responsibility of government to Parliament and to the electorate. If, on a subject of this importance, the government were to propose one course and a referendum choose the other, then, unless the Government promptly resigned, they would be able thereafter to say, whatever happened: 'Well, don't blame us, it is no fault of ours; we wanted to do one thing, but you decided to do the other; so, ladies and gentlemen, you have only yourselves to blame.' The result of that would be, quite literally, irresponsible government.

Secondly, there are many people who believe – though I am not one of them, as I shall presently show – that the decision about Britain entering the Common Market ought to depend on what are called the 'terms' which can be negotiated. Obviously, from this point of view it is not possible to have a decision, yes or no, in advance. On the other hand, once the 'terms' had been negotiated and worked out in detail, then, as with a treaty or any other international instrument, they could not be rejected unless the government itself were defeated. Only close and continuous debate, in Parliament and the country, during the progress of the negotiations could ensure that the 'terms' which were accepted were such as to satisfy opinion.

However, just because a referendum will not answer, it does not follow that the issue of the Common Market ought to be kept under wraps at a general election. On the contrary, in my opinion it is a duty which the electorate ought to exact from every candidate, to 'come clean' on this question. If his support of entry is unconditional, well and good, let him make that plain and the electors know where they stand. If he believes that the case for or against depends on the conditions, then let him indicate – not of course in detail but in broad outline – what the conditions are on which he would support entry. It is no use just saying: 'We will negotiate and see what terms can be had.' You are entitled to know what sort of terms are in mind, and how they will be judged. Are the terms to do with transitional arrangements, or are they permanent? Are they economic, or are they also political? If they are economic, are they concerned with agriculture or with currency or with taxation, and how high a price, broadly, would be regarded as acceptable?

There is, however, a third category of candidate, whose opposition to entry into the Common

Market is unconditional and based on the nature of the Common Market itself: he too ought to declare his position.

This is the right way for public opinion on such a subject to find expression: the electorate ought to know, if they elect a candidate, where he will range himself on this issue. And let no one say that Members are mere lobby-fodder, and that a government will get its way, no matter. It is only a year or so since, on a subject where public opinion was much less deeply exercised – the future of the second chamber – a major government measure, to which the official Opposition was at worst benevolently neutral, was destroyed by the determined action of private members on both sides of the House. I would not care to put much money on entry to the Common Market coming about if a substantial minority of Members on the government side were pledged to oppose it. In any case the maximum ventilation of the whole issue is something to which the Conservative Party is committed. Mr. Heath never spoke truer words than when he said that 'the greatest possible mistake would be for the British people to go into this without themselves realizing the full implications'.

What the 'full implications' are, becomes clearer on the side of the Economic Community with almost every week that passes. I myself believe that those implications are already firm enough for many people to make up their minds where they stand.

What has emerged with startling rapidity in the recent past is how profoundly political, how far-reaching and how imminent those implications are. Six months ago, I quoted the then head of the E.E.C. Commission when he predicted that the Community would have a common currency and a common parliament elected on universal suffrage before 1980. Yet even as recently as six months ago, people were inclined to treat such a prediction as the personal pipe-dream of an enthusiast. That is no longer possible. In the last fortnight the countries of the Six have not only adopted the target of a common currency before 1980 but have agreed that as from now 'whatever the International Monetary Fund may decide on greater flexibility for exchange rates, the Six will not accept any widening of the present permitted margins of fluctuation in dealings between their own currencies'. This was rightly described as 'the first step towards creating a common currency'.

I am aware that this may all sound very technical and financial. Indeed, it is not. On the contrary, it affects everyone directly. This election to a large extent is about prices, about wages, about inflation, even about balance of payments. If Britain were a member of a Common Market with a common currency, a British general election would have as little to do with those subjects as the municipal elections, and the British parliament would have as little control over them as the Staffordshire County Council has today. Money is managed by governments, and the management of money determines wages, prices, employment and the whole economy. What else have we been arguing about for the last three weeks – or the last six years, for that matter? A single currency means a single government, and that single government would be the government whose policies determined every aspect of economic life. In the Common Market that government would not be a British government; it would be a continental government, and the British electorate would be a comparatively small minority of the electorate to which that government was responsible.

Remember, we are not talking about a remote future. We are thinking, let us say, of the next general election but one. At that election, if the Economic Community survives and develops – presumably there is no point in this whole debate unless we assume that will happen – and if Britain is part of the Community, then my fellow candidates and I, even if we are candidates for the European and not the British Parliament, will have a very different tale to tell you. Prices (let us imagine) have been going up by five or six per cent a year, and you the electors are justifiably angry. You want to turn out of office those responsible for this, much as you are going to turn out the present Labour Government later this week. But we, my fellow candidates and I, will say to you: 'Sorry; these are the results of the policy followed by the European government, which controls the European currency. We have done, and we shall do, our best; but this is how the majority in the Community insist on having it.'

You will agree that it would be a tremendous step for this country to transfer to a unit in which it will be a permanent minority the control of its economic life – from unemployment to taxation, from prices to development policy. Yet even this does not exhaust the 'full implications' of entry into the Common Market. The twin argument which is urged in favour of entry is that, especially with the prospective reduction of American forces and commitment, it would give the countries of Western Europe a defensive capability which mere alliance does not. As the German ex-Minister, Herr Strauss, put it recently, 'Europe must become a political unit with a stronger defence capability'; for the continental politician often does not duck the realities, as too many British politicians do. The condition of a stronger defence capability is a common government, a common government which will decide for the whole of Western Europe how much of its resources are to be applied to defence and how those resources are to be used. Now, we in this country can take different views, as the Labour and Conservative parties do, of the relative priorities of education and defence; we may argue about whether defence should absorb 10 or 7 or 5 per cent of our national income. What I cannot believe is that the people of the United Kingdom ought to submit, or would submit, to these questions being decided, and to themselves being taxed and conscripted – and how can conscription not be involved? – by the government of a political unit in which they were a minority. Even less, if possible, do I believe that they should or would surrender the keys of the ultimate defence of these islands to a sovereign authority of continental character, continental location and continental outlook.

For twenty years a majority of the people of this constituency have given to me the most precious privilege that a man can seek in a free country, the opportunity to be heard; to be heard in Parliament, but also, because of the unique nature and prestige of Parliament, to be heard outside. In recent years the voice which you have given me has carried further and further, until, without office or any other position or assistance except what you gave me, I have been able to be heard by my fellow countrymen from one end of the country to the other, and the response and echo has returned to me from hundreds of thousands of homes.

Tonight I mean to use that voice to say one thing and one thing only; but it is the one thing which most concerns the future of this nation and the well-being, not merely material, of all its inhabitants. In forty-eight hours they have one word to say, 'Yea' or 'Nay'; but in that word and its consequences are embraced all that they would wish for their tomorrow. There is, it seems to me, too great a danger that the gravity and (in some respects) the finality of that decision may not everywhere be realized, and that indifference or heedlessness or distraction could obscure it. We must regain, before the die is cast, the view of those great simplicities in the light of which the nation's decision ought to be taken.

In saying to you, and through you to the country: 'Vote, and vote Tory', I have at least one accidental

advantage. It is not such as anyone would go looking for; but having it, I claim the right to use it. I
have no personal gain to expect from the outcome,
other than that of any other citizen. I am not among
those candidates at this election who can look forward with assurance, or at least with hope, to re-
taining or to achieving political office under the
Crown according as the result of the election in-
clines one way or the other. Whatever might have
been obscure or undefined about the policies of the
Conservative Party, this at least has been made
crystal clear, over and over again, by the Leader of
the Party, that if there is a Conservative Government after Thursday, I shall not be a member of it.
The place to which I ask the electors of Wolverhampton South West to return me is that place,
somewhere about the middle of the third bench
above the gangway, which I have customarily occupied during more than half my twenty years in
Parliament. The most I can hope is to be sitting
there again – on one side of the House or the other.
Nor have I received in the recent past from men
who will form a Conservative Cabinet even the ordinary loyalties and courtesies that prevail generally between colleagues in the same cause. Not for
them to repudiate attacks upon me which were unfounded, and which they knew to be unfounded.
Not for them to place upon my words and argu-
ments the more favourable, or the most obvious,
construction, or even to accept my own assertion of
my own meaning. Not for them to protest when in
the House of Commons language has been used
about me, and insults have been cast, the obscenity

of which has lowered the dignity of Parliament itself.

No wonder that, by word and letter, from all parts of the country, a tide, which rose and fell but never ceased, of encouragement and reassurance has flowed in to me from strangers, from the general public, from the ordinary people of this country; for the instinct of fairness is one of the deep and characteristic instincts of this nation. No wonder that when this election came, electors have been writing to me, and have been saying to Conservative candidates in the constituences, that they would not be voting Conservative 'because Enoch Powell would not be in a Conservative Government' or 'because of the way Enoch Powell has been treated'.

It is precisely because of all this that I claim the right at this moment to say to these people; to say to all those who, silently or vocally, have approved and supported what I have had to say and to do in my public life; to say, indeed, to the whole electorate: 'Don't be fooled; don't fool yourselves, and don't let anyone else fool you. This election is not about me, not about Enoch Powell, not about any other named variety. This election is about you and your future and your children's future and your country's future.' Not surprisingly, considering the level of triviality at which most of this election has been spent, a great part of the electorate have been drugged into supposing that it is no more than a presidential contest of personalities, and that they are just being invited to decide if they prefer the country and the economy, which will be much the same anyhow, to be presided over by a man with a pipe or a man with a boat. But this is not a presidential election. This is not a pop contest. This is a decision not between two individuals but between two futures for Britain, futures irrevocably, irreversibly different.

If a socialist majority is returned on Thursday, then before another three or four years are over, the ownership and control of the state will have been extended, by one means or another, over the greater part of British industry and business. Even in the outgoing months of the old parliament, even during the very election campaign itself, public money has been used to buy ownership and control in one major industry after another: in machine tools, in Rolls-Royce, in Cammell Laird, in British Leyland, in the exploration and exploitation of petroleum in the seas around these islands after private enterprise and risk had first revealed and brought to use that unexpected asset.

Anyone who supposes this 'take-over' will stop must be deaf and blind. Give this Socialist Government the opportunity, and the process will be speeded up and pushed forward with a ruthlessness that will accelerate as the parts of British industry where the bureaucrat does not yet have the upper hand diminish. The point is eventually reached when the remaining elements of free enterprise, realizing that they are in the power of the state-controlled undertakings from which they buy and to which they sell, give up the unequal struggle and succumb. This is what socialism is about. This is the 'capture of the commanding heights' in the old-fashioned language of the pioneers. This is what another three or four years of Labour government is intended to accomplish.

Another process will be going on at the same time. The young, the enterprising, the independent in mind and spirit, will be able to read the signs. In increasing numbers they will conclude that a socialist Britain is no place in which to lead their own lives, to bring up their children, and to foresee their descendants' future. At this moment about 130,000 British-born men, women and children emigrate yearly from this country. I would be guilty of my besetting fault of understatement if I described that as 'a trickle'; but however you care to describe it, the flow would broaden into a flood as more people saw the writing on the wall and understood what their future would be in a socialist Britain.

I am not just talking about freedom and enterprise in economic terms. I am talking also of individual liberty. Already in the last four years socialism has been forming up to withdraw the fundamental freedoms of personal and family decision; for it is not only the economy but society itself that these men intend to bring under the power and management of the state. In another four years who dare be sure that parents will be allowed to choose and to buy the education for their children that they think best? to choose and to buy the care in health and in sickness that they think best? to make provision and to save in the manner that they think best for their retirement and their families? All these freedoms have already been under attack in the parliament which is ended. In the new parliament, if it contains a socialist majority, the assault will be carried forward. I say again that there is a point where the best of the nation in all walks of life would give up the unequal struggle and either acquiesce in the managed uniformity of a socialist state or go where they will be free.

Listen, then; for there comes a time when it is too late to listen. On Thursday let none delude you that you are choosing between individuals, or that the questions you decide will come up again in the same form, the same circumstances, a few years ahead, should you dislike the outcome now. On Thursday your vote is about a Britain that, with all its faults and failings, is still free, and great because it is free. On Thursday your vote decides whether that freedom shall survive or not. You dare not entrust it to any government but a Conservative government.

On going to Press, although the post mortem of Harris Poll on the election was not complete, the following preliminary conclusions 'on the Powell issue' had been reached, which are printed here by permission of Louis Harris Research Ltd. and the *Daily Express*.

'Although Mr. Powell may have been doing damage to Mr. Heath's reputation as a strong leader of his party during the campaign, we found it highly probable that on balance Powell helped the Conservative cause rather than damaged it. Race and immigration were not among the leading issues of the election but our evidence shows that, if anything, they were ones which tended to help the Conservatives. At the same time we found that the strongest bedrock of Mr. Powell's support came from the skilled working class, which comprises one third of the total population: they normally support Labour in strong numbers of course, but many of them had only recently returned to the Labour fold and their support was fragile and easily prised away.

Finally, we found that Mr. Powell had a very strong televisual appeal during the election.

All these factors led us to the conclusion that Anthony Wedgwood-Benn, by bringing out the Powell issue, committed one of the main blunders of the campaign. Mr. Heath on the other hand played this issue about right; he was under heavy pressure, one week away from polling day, to have Powell removed from the Conservative party, but such evidence as we have indicates that he would have lost more than he gained by doing this.'

THE GUILTY MADMEN OF WHITEHALL

By Andrew G. Elliot

London Evening News: '... takes a swing at the Whitehall "madmen" ... he has a ready wit, a rapier-like "sock it to me" turn of phrase which makes the welter of increased taxation seem side-splitting mirth. It is a must ...'

Sunday Mail: 'Scot lashes out at the Cabinet ... He is everyman's lobbyist ... fires shot after shot into Mr Wilson's ship of state ... sensational ...'

Probably the hardest hitting political book ever written. Scores of readers have written to tell the publisher they have bought the book in dozens, hundreds and one man even a thousand to give to friends and acquaintances.

The book deals with Grade A, B and C Socialists ... The Prevalence Of Political Paranoia ... Fifty-Six Million Planners ... Idiotic Taxation ... Britain's Biggest Industry – Avoiding Tax ... The Secret Socialist Target ... The Two Flops – Education and Health ... Gold For the Whizz Kids ... The Jackpotters ... Up the Socialist Spout ... and goes on to tell you the things that you can do.

Readers' comments 'As I read your book flying over the Atlantic I leapt out of my seat for joy.'

Another reader 'Your book raised my blood pressure but I bought 6 more copies.'

Another reader 'I have read your book 5 times; I want to shout its contents from the house tops.'

Another Paperfront – uniform with this book

PERSUASIVE SPEAKING

By W. George Jehan

Uniquely designed to emphasize and explain the author's eleven principles of persuasive speaking. This is a practical instruction book which the publishers believe to be the outstanding book on the subject.

P.T.O.

The eleven principles

First Principle: **Unity and steadfastness of purpose.**
Second Principle: **Be forthright and newsworthy.**
Third Principle: **Create a vivid picture.**
Fourth Principle: **Avoid abstract phrases.**
Fifth Principle: **Generate true emotion.**
Sixth Principle: **Meet your audience on a common plane.**
Seventh Principle: **Reveal your emotions.**
Eighth Principle: **Project your emotions.**
Ninth Principle: **Always speak extempore.**
Tenth Principle: **Keep to one theme.**
Eleventh Principle: **Don't violate the unity of your speech.**

Insist on this Paperfront – uniform with this book

The Right Way to

CONDUCT MEETINGS, CONFERENCES and DISCUSSIONS

By H. M. Taylor and A. G. Mears

The book chosen by Her Majesty's Government for the English Language Book Society Series.

People throughout the world recognize this as the standard work on the subject.

Uniform with this book

From All Booksellers, If Difficulty Direct
ELLIOT RIGHT WAY BOOKS, KINGSWOOD, SURREY, U.K.